The Land of

Folk Songs and Settings of

edited by Mic

Dedicated to my ve... ...iend
"Bruno"

Published by:
Michael Raven,
Yew Tree Cottage, Jug Bank, Ashley,
Market Drayton, Shropshire,
TF9 4NJ
Telephone: 01630 672304
E-mail: michael.raven@virgin.net
Web site:
http://freespace.virgin.net/michael.raven/index.htm

First Edition: Summer 1999

Music setting: Michael Raven using Finale 98

Printed by: Cox and Wyman, Reading

Front cover picture:
Glowed with tints of Evening Hours
by Joseph Farquharson (1846-1935)

ISBN: 0 906114 32 2

Preface

THIS is a collection of songs in which I have had a hand as composer, author or arranger. They span the period 1964 to 1999 and have been categorised giving primary regard to the words. I have spoken to many singers and song-writers over the years and almost all agree that the lyrics that are the most important element in a song. However, this does seem to be a modern opinion. Until the middle of the 20th century it was the tune makers who stole the glory. John Dowland and Franz Schubert were musicians, not poets.

I am an instrumentalist but have worked with a variety of singers, from the gentle and lyrical to the strong and rhythmical, both as a solo accompanist and a member of groups. This is reflected in the songs I have worked on. They range from gritty Black Country broadsides to the delicate soul searchings of Victorian poets, and from ancient epic ballads to songs written but yesterday.

Incidentally, it is often harder to find and fit a traditional melody to the lyrics of a poet than to compose an original tune. The benefit, of course, is that a good folk aire has qualities that even the most talented of modern composers can rarely match, let alone my humble self. What is more, such melodies do not inherently require instrumental accompaniment and sound effective sung a capella. The same is rarely true of art song settings, and in modern popular music the instrumental backing is very often more important than the song itself.

Related to this is the drum machine mentality of relentless rhythms. This is very much a modern pop music development and alien to both classical and folk music where a degree of flexibility is called for. Indeed, interpretation as a whole is noticeably absent in the performances of many folk artistes who largely ignore the use of variations in volume level, tone colouring and tempo.

I have given the chords which I use as the basis of my arrangements for guitar, but these are only guides. I usually insert many passing harmonies and frequently play the melodies above them. Drones are often effective, especially in the more spritely tunes where the melody note/bass drone combination creates delicate and shifting harmonies that cannot be improved upon and which often lend a modality that can be acheived in no other way. Rhythmically strummed chords are rarely the best way of accompanying traditional material, though singer/song-writers often follow modern styles and use harmonic progressions as the basis of their music.

Finally, readers should feel free to alter anything in a song with which they feel uncomfortable. Use completeley different tunes, change words or leave out verses, if you please. This is how some of our most beautiful folk songs have been created. M. R.

Contents

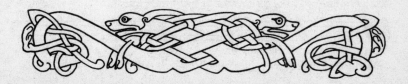

Belle Star and Jesse James

Words and music: Michael Raven

Some - time I'm lone - ly, some - times I'm blue; Some - times I just don't know what I'm gon - na do Be - cause he's gone,——— Jes - se's gone. Sit - ting here cry - ing 'cause he's gone,——— Wish - ing I was dy - ing 'cause he's gone;——— Jes - se's gone.

Secondary chorus used after third and fifth verse choruses

Li li li li, li li li li li li li, Li li li li, li li li li li li li.

Sometimes I'm lonely, sometimes I'm blue;
Sometimes I just don't know what I'm gonna do
Because he's gone, Jesse's gone.

Chorus:
Sitting here crying 'cause he's gone;
Wishing I was dying 'cause he's gone,
Jesse's gone.

Belle Star they call me, the Lily of the West,
But I would gladly die for the man I love the best,
And now he's gone, Jesse's gone.

Well, eight men have loved me, and loved me so well,
But Jesse James the only one was loved by Belle,
And now he's gone, Jesse's gone.

Li li li li, li li li li li li li li,
Li li li li, li li li li li li li li.

I remember Glendale and how he did ride,
Ten days and nights to be by my side,
And now he's gone, Jesse's gone.

I'm goin' away, now, leaving in the Fall;
Leaving on that train they call the Canonball
From Washington to Arkinsaw.

Li li li li, li li li li li li li li,
Li li li li, li li li li li li li li.

Twenty Years

Words and music: Michael Raven

Of friends I have so many now,
And laughter I do know so well,
But joy my heart will never know,
And I have love no tongue can tell.

Oh I may wish for good fortune,
And sing a gay and a merry song,
But dreams and songs are like false love:
One day they're here and then they're gone.

No mind can know how deep my sorrow;
No mind can know my fondest dream;
No mind can know a dagger bright,
So cold, so sharp, so cold, so clean.

There sits a bird on yonder tree,
Sings a song and it pleases me,
Sings a song and sings farewell,
And I have love no words can tell.

For twenty years the corn grew high;
For twenty years I've told the lie;
Twenty years have passed my love
Since I did shed your precious blood.

Go You Down with Pride

Words: Michael Raven; music: Joan Mills

So feel the sun upon your face, and hide that aching sigh,
And tell those heroes yet unborn how your dear comrades died.
Lest they forget tell them the debt and how the price was paid -
How they rose up, alive at dawn; by eve, Last Post was played.

So go you down with pride, old men, so go you down with pride.
And when the demons of the night parade by your bedside
Rise up, salute your long lost dead, who once did walk this land,
And feel the warmth old ghosts can give, and shake them by the hand.

Flowers of Picardy

Words and music: Michael Raven

Now I am old, love, how the time do fly,
Now all my friends are gone, beneath the earth they lie.
I'll not hang my head, love, shed you not a tear;
Winter follows Summer, it's the turning of the year.

I remember well, love, the day you went away,
How tall you stood and handsome, how bright the band did play.
My very heart was breaking, and free the tears did flow,
And now you lie in Picardy where the wild flowers grow.

There are pinks and posies, calendine and rue,
Marigolds and daisies, all a part of you.
Fresh the fields of Flanders, oh, so dear to me;
When I die just let me lie in the Plains of Picardy.

White, white the snow, love, blue, blue the sky;
Green, green the grass, love, the ground where you do lie.
Black, black the day, love, that you did cross the sea,
Now all I can have of you are the Flowers of Picardy.

Small rains are falling, I hear them call your name;
Small winds are whispering, "He'll come home again."
But my ears are deaf now to such taunting lies;
All I hear is silence and the gentle breeze that sighs.

Johnny, lovely Johnny, I'm coming home to you,
I'll put on the green dress, my little coat of blue,
I'll bring that poem you wrote me, the one that made me cry,
Happy now I am to be, once more by your side.

Funeral Hymn

Words and music: Michael Raven

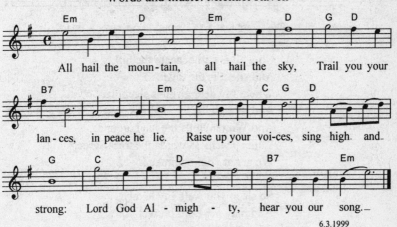

All hail the moun-tain, all hail the sky, Trail you your
lan-ces, in peace he lie. Raise up your voi-ces, sing high and
strong: Lord God Al-migh-ty, hear you our song.—

6.3.1999

Dreary the long night, cold is the clay,
Life is but a moment, death will not stay.
Silent the Winter, Summer soon come,
Lighten our darkness, His will be done.

Now All is Still

Words and music: Michael Raven

Now all is still beneath the hill, And si-lent is— the town, Where my dear girl lies sleep-ing. And— though the wind blows cold, And— Win-ter chills the land a-round, With— speech-less words the trees a-gree, We are at your com-mand.

Now all is still beneath the hill,
And silent is the town,
Where my dear girl lies sleeping.
And though the wind blows cold,
And Winter chills the land around,
With speechless words the trees agree,
We are at your command.

So sleep you well, my lovely,
And may the Lord protect you
From the dark and fiercesome night;
And now the curse of life
Has shorn away the painted veil
I have come to say my last farewell,
Oh fare thee well, my love.

Slain in Egypt

Words and music: Michael Raven

I am sor-ry, dear Sir, to— take of your time, And so I'll be brief:— I— ask of the— line, And of Priv-ate John-son, my eld-est dear son; He's a good lad at heart, Sir, and— bright as— the sun.

30.7.1999

I am sorry, dear Sir, to take of your time,
And so I'll be brief: I ask of the line,
And of Private Johnson, my eldest dear son;
He's a good lad at heart, Sir, and bright as the sun.

Just tell him the Harvest was Home yesterday,
And Sarah is due now and how she do pray
That John he come home when the war it is won,
And work on the farm and forgo the gun.

Just tell me he's well, that's all I do ask,
For you must have many more pressing a task.
The reply, when it came, was "John he was slain;
Enclosed is his watch and his father's gold chain."

Oh how I do wish I'd the strength of a man.
I'd drink and I'd swear and march through the sand,
Through the fires of all Hell to Egypt's dark shore.
In midnights of madness I'd rant and I'd roar.

Convict's Complaint

Words and music: Michael Raven

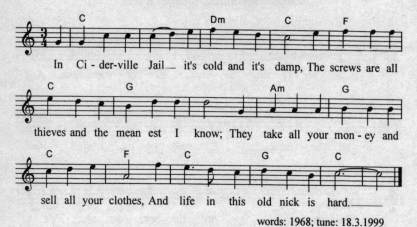

In Ci-der-ville Jail— it's cold and it's damp, The screws are all thieves and the mean est I know; They take all your mon-ey and sell all your clothes, And life in this old nick is hard.——

words: 1968; tune: 18.3.1999

In Ciderville Jail it's cold and it's damp,
The screws are all thieves and the meanest I know;
They take all your money and sell all your clothes,
And life in this old nick is hard.
There's bars on the windows and bolts on the door;
There's bugs in your mattress and rats on the floor.
They chase you and haze you till you can't take no more,
And life in this old nick is hard.

They wake you at six and you roll up your bed;
They march you to breakfast and when you've been fed
They march you in threes to the lousy mail shed,
And life in this old nick is hard.
They count you and curse you by three and by two;
They're counting machines with nowt else to do
But count you and curse you from midnight to noon,
And life in this old nick is hard.

The jingle and jangle of keys in the lock,
The cries in the night from them down in the Block;
And even the priest has keys chained to his frock,
And life in this old nick is hard.
The preacher's a good man and good at his job,
He rants and he raves and condemns us who rob,
But his orders come from the Governor, not God,
And life in this old nick is hard.

For ten hours a day you sew mail for the Queen,
They work you and slave you like you're a machine;
Your fingers all blisters, no Doc to be seen,
And life in this old nick is hard.
I've cut grass with scissors and painted coal white,
Been beaten and kicked for two days and a night.
They're tin gods and tyrants, they ain't worth a damn,
And life in this old nick is hard.

The Brewer's Lady

Words and music: Michael Raven

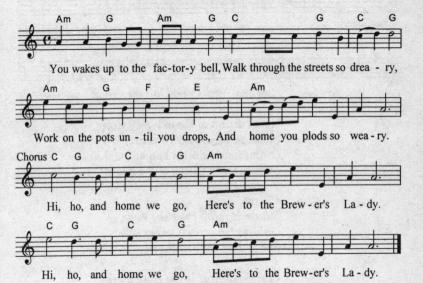

You wakes up to the fac-tor-y bell, Walk through the streets so drea - ry,

Work on the pots un - til you drops, And home you plods so wea - ry.

Hi, ho, and home we go, Here's to the Brew - er's La - dy.

Hi, ho, and home we go, Here's to the Brew - er's La - dy.

Sunday morn and the dogs we take,
Up on the hill right early.
My little Tess beat Old Tom's Bess,
And he came home right surly.

Come July we're off to Rhyl,
Off to the shores so sandy,
Wife and kids and Heaven forbids
No drinking on a Sunday.

Winter time is bitter here,
High on Hanley's hill, Sir,
Winds they moan, chill to the bone,
The cold up here can kill, Sir.

Queen of the Night

Words and music: Michael Raven

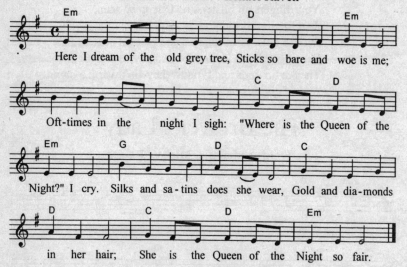

Here I dream of the old grey tree, Sticks so bare and woe is me;
Oft-times in the night I sigh: "Where is the Queen of the
Night?" I cry. Silks and sa-tins does she wear, Gold and dia-monds
in her hair; She is the Queen of the Night so fair.

Here I dream of the old grey tree,
Sticks so bare and woe is me;
Ofttimes in the night I sigh:
"Where is the Queen of the Night?" I cry.

Chorus:
Silks and satins does she wear,
Gold and diamonds in her hair;
She is the Queen of the Night so fair.

Crackle of frost in the Autumn sky,
See the blackbird oh so shy;
To the Hell of Heaven I go,
There is no peace in the ground below.

She has charmed and torn my soul,
Raged the fire with golden coal;
I care not if I live or die:
"Where is the Queen of the night?" I cry.

Give me a shroud of Tangier hue,
Ten tall Arabs of noble brood;
Set them each with a silver spade;
Dig for me the deepest grave.

Is My Dear Lord Asleep?

Words and music: Michael Raven

I changed the wa-ter in-to wine, I sowed the seeds of love di-vine, And gave the light to the blind of sight, And all in the world was right.

I changed the water into wine,
I sowed the seeds of love divine,
And gave the light to the blind of sight,
And all in the world was right.

He made the moon and the stars above,
He made the wren and the turtle dove,
But now I weep at my father's feet.
Is my dear lord asleep?

Out on the sea hear the wild wind's roar,
So far from home, so far from shore.
"Oh why, oh why," the sailors cry,
"Must we languish here and die?"

And here is a pretty girl, the world at her feet,
Cut down in her prime and half the world weeps,
And there but for the grace of God go I,
In cold, cold clay to lie.

And high on a hill by a desert shore
Stand English knights, twelve hundred score.
With sword and shield they will not yield,
Now lie on a foreign field.

He made the moon and the stars above,
He made the wren and the turtle dove,
But now I weep at my father's feet.
Is my dear lord asleep?

Tim Evans' Dance

Words and music: Michael Raven

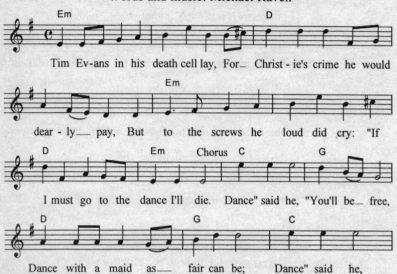

Tim Ev-ans in his death cell lay, For_ Christ-ie's crime he would
dear-ly_ pay, But to the screws he loud did cry: "If
I must go to the dance I'll die. Dance" said he, "You'll be_ free,
Dance with a maid as_ fair can be; Dance" said he,
"You'll be_ free." And he danced to his death with his Gip-sy Lee.

He found him a flute with the sweetest sound,
Played him a tune and danced it around;
Danced to the Dawn and the Evening Sun,
And danced to the Night when his work was done.

He danced with the Judge and his eyes shone bright,
"You are so wrong and I am right.
We'll meet again in Heaven my friend;
Of this dance there can be no end."

He danced with a screw in his coat so blue,
Danced him a reel or a jig or two,
Whirled him and twirled him and leapt so high,
Till: "You're of the Devil," the screw did cry.

He danced all the way to his grim death cell,
Danced with the Hangman and he danced well,
Danced with the Priest and told a good joke,
And dancing he died on the Hangman's rope.

English Lanes

Words Michael Raven (verses 2, 3, and 4) and Greta Brydges Jones
(verse 1); music: Michael Raven

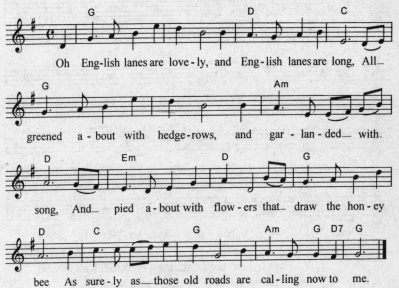

Oh English lanes are lovely, and English lanes are long,
All greened about with hedgerows, and garlanded with song,
And pied about with flowers that draw the honey bee
As surely as those old roads are calling now to me.

They wander down through Wiltshire, at Castle Combe they sigh,
And Shropshire lads in Ludlow all smile as they pass by.
They'll dance you down to Devon, to Cornwall's creeks and coves,
And show you things to treasure, and tell you tales long told.

They roam around the lowlands of Norfolk to the sea,
And make you long for England, wherever you may be;
And when your days are darkened, and you can take no more,
These lanes will lead you homeward, they answer when you call.

The flowered lanes of Springtime, they cheer the traveller's day;
And fields of corn in Summer, they wave him on his way;
But the tired lanes of Autumn, they lull his soul to sleep,
And guide the winds of Winter, their harvest for to reap.

Love is a Wonder

Words and music: Michael Raven

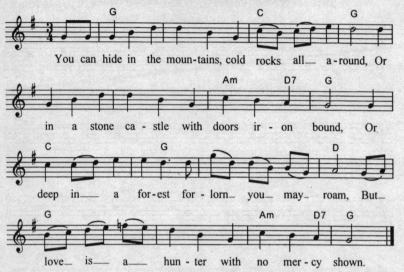

You can hide in the moun-tains, cold rocks all— a-round, Or in a stone ca - stle with doors ir - on bound, Or deep in— a for-est for - lorn— you— may— roam, But— love— is— a— hun - ter with no mer - cy shown.

13.10.1998

You can hide in the mountains, cold rocks all around,
Or in a stone castle with doors iron bound,
Or deep in a forest forlorn you may roam,
But love is a hunter with no mercy shown.

You cannot escape her, her claws are so sharp
They'll rip you asunder and tear out your heart.
Then she will caress you and sweetly will sing,
Until she deserts you and sorrow is king.

For love is a wonder and ever was so,
And love she's a lady who never says "No".
She laughs in the sunlight and cries in the night;
She's all things to all men, and all men's delight.

She'll dance you to heaven, then dance you to hell.
She'll whisper sweet nothings, sweet lies she will tell,
And when all is perfect, and you are content,
She'll bite like a serpent, your world she will rent.

For love is a wonder and ever was so,
And love she's a lady who never says "No".
She laughs in the sunlight and cries in the night;
She's all things to all men, and all men's delight.

Maid from the Northlands

Words and music: Michael Raven

I can tell you're from the North-lands; were you born in Don-e-gal? I can hear the sound of Sum-mer in the rise and in the fall, Of the gen-tle voice of eve-ning at the dy-ing of the day, I can hear the hills in mourn-ing for the day you went a-way. The gen-tle voice of eve-ning at the dy-ing of the day; I can hear the hills in mourn-ing for the day you went a-way.

I can hear the curlew crying on the cliffs above the sea,
I can hear the grasses sighing when you turn and smile at me,
And the cottage fire is burning, the lark it sounds so clear,
And though you are so far away you are forever near.

In your eyes I see the sunlight, how it wakes the darkened shore.
The wild geese now are homeward bound across the moonlit moor,
And the cottage door is open and there's your mother dear,
And though you are so far away she is forever near.

Biker's Song

Words and music: Michael Raven

I ride the road, I'm as free as the air,
No one to worry and no one to care,
No one to love me and no one to share,
Like the beast in the field, like the fox in his lair.

I'm not the singer, I never wrote a song,
I'm not the dancer who danced all night long.
I am the rider who rode on and on,
An eagle of freedom, a righter of wrong.

Oh! Give me a Norton 500 to ride,
I will not shelter and I will not hide.
I will burn rubber until I do die,
No one will grieve me and no one will cry.

We ride the high mountains, the valleys so deep;
We're sons of Satan who never sleep.
We'll ride for ever and for ever more,
Live by the rules not of Man but of Law.

Crewe to Carlisle and to Rochester shore,
A thousand night riders, a thousand or more,
Torches a-blazing, a sight for to see,
The waters are burning, the spirit set free.

Sarabande

Words and music: Michael Raven

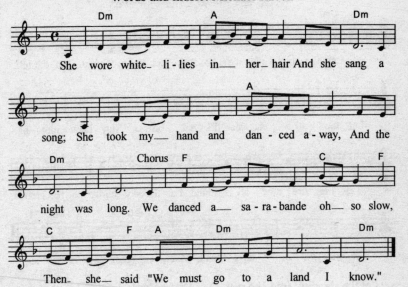

She wore white lilies in her hair
And she sang a song;
She took my hand and danced away,
And the night was long.

The trees grew high, the trees grew low,
And the sun did sing;
Scarlet rain fell from the sky,
With a hollow ring.

We came to a stream where silver salmon flew,
And the corn grew high.
A lazy snake lay dreaming in the sun,
As two came by.

We met an old man dressed in green,
And he spoke to me.
"Come my son and dance with me,
And your fair lady."

The sun had set, the night grew cold,
As we danced away;
I was a king and she but a maid,
But death won't stay.

Octopus Dancing

Words and music: Michael Raven

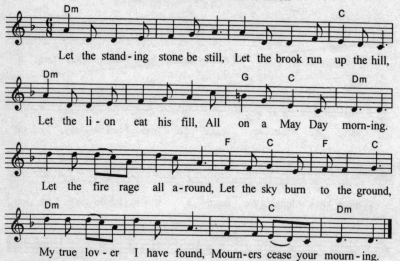

Let the stand-ing stone be still, Let the brook run up the hill,

Let the li-on eat his fill, All on a May Day morn-ing.

Let the fire rage all a-round, Let the sky burn to the ground,

My true lov-er I have found, Mourn-ers cease your mourn-ing.

Let the standing stone be still,
Let the brook run up the hill,
Let the lion eat his fill,
All on a May Day morning.
Let the fire rage all around,
Let the sky burn to the ground,
My true lover I have found,
Mourners cease your mourning.

Over mountain tracks we stride,
Rocks and rivers never lied,
Hear the song that never died,
The lark so sweet ascending.
Take your axe and take your gun,
When your day's work it is done,
When your battle it is won,
Watch the night descending.

Distant bells do dimly ring,
To their faith the faithful cling,
Singing songs unto their king,
Songs of love and glory.
Then the door bursts open, then
In ride dark and weathered men,
Sword in hand into God's den,
To sell their Christian story.

Riddle me this and riddle me that,
What is wet and midnight black?
What's the point in turning back
All on the road to nowhere?
Zanzibar or far Cathay,
Get you there all in one day,
But there is a price to pay,
"But why," you ask, "should I care?"

Why don't we just jack it in?
Take us off for a jolly spin
On the back of a gay dolphin,
And wander on the ocean.
Visit whales and say "Hello",
Tea with turtles, then we go
Octopus dancing down below,
Oh what a lovely notion.

My Old Friend

Words and music Michael Raven except verse 1 by Harvey Andrews

Old friend, my— old friend, Now you've reached your jour-ney's end, All e-ter-nal life— to spend: Sleep you well,— my old friend. Sleep— you well, my— old friend, Now— you've reached your jour - ney's— end.

Old friend, my old friend,
Now you've reached your journey's end,
All eternal life to spend:
Sleep you well, my old friend.

Time there was when we ran free,
Through the greenwood, o'er the lea,
No thought then of what might be:
Sleep you well, my old friend.

Now I laugh and cry alone;
Summer days are cold as stone
Since the day I brought you home:
Sleep you well, my old friend.

Often now I stand and stare,
And think of times beyond all care,
And wish to God that you were there:
Sleep you well, my old friend.

For Pirate,
died 7.11.1997

Short time here and long time dead,
Time to think on things unsaid,
Oh, how soon the years have fled:
Sleep you well, my old friend.

Sailor Home

Words and music: Michael Raven

21.9.1999

There are storm clouds to the lee,
And a dark and a rolling sea,
But none too soon, 'neath the dark-eyed moon,
From her I am set free.

For I am a sailor home;
Home from the raging foam,
And now that the sea has done with me
No longer will I roam.

There's many a night gone by,
When all alone I'd lie,
And dream of you, the things we'd do,
That fate would us deny.

I'd watch the sun sink low,
And idle talk would flow,
And friends with me would disagree,
But laughing we'd roll home.

I've sailed the ocean round,
From 'Frisco to Plymouth Sound,
But now that's done, my race is run,
And I am homeward bound.

I've a cottage by the shore,
And now do little more,
Than gaze at the sea that still calls me,
With the girl I do adore.

Sweet Robinette

Words and music: Michael Raven

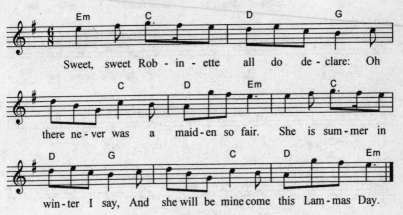

Sweet, sweet Rob - in - ette all do de - clare: Oh there ne - ver was a maid - en so fair. She is sum - mer in win - ter I say, And she will be mine come this Lam - mas Day.

Sweet, sweet Robinette all do declare:
Oh there never was a maiden so fair.
She is summer in winter I say,
And she will be mine come this Lammas Day.

Eyes she has as black as a sloe,
And her sweet lips as red as a rose;
Sweet, sweet Robinette all do declare:
Oh there never was a maiden so fair.

Dancing Delilah

Words and music: Michael Raven

Dancing Delilah they called her,
Dancing, dancing all the day;
Dancing Delilah they called her,
Dancing she stole their hearts away.
She danced the rhumba and fandango,
She danced the czardas and koombay.
Dancing Delilah they called her,
Dancing she stole their hearts away.

I saw her first in Sarajevo,
Dancing in a café in the dark,
Danced to the rhythm of the shell-fire,
People they were dying in the park.
Then it was Paris in the evening,
Swaying down a sunlit boulevard,
Laughing with friends to the casino,
She always had a winning card.

But I have seen her in the morning,
I've seen that tear in her eye,
I've seen a heart that was breaking,
I've heard that long and lonely sigh.
I've seen her dance up to Moscow,
Hamburg, then Prague and Amsterdam;
Died in a bar in Barcelona,
Drunk, old and no one gave a damn.

Nailmakers' Lament

Words and music: Michael Raven

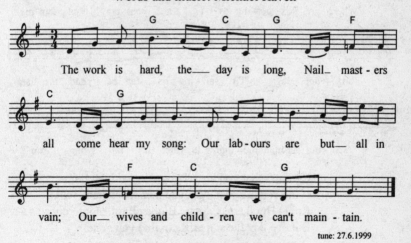

The work is hard, the day is long, Nail mast-ers
all come hear my song: Our lab-ours are but all in
vain; Our wives and child-ren we can't main-tain.

tune: 27.6.1999

In eighteen hundred and fifty-two
You broke our strike, our Union too,
And now machines rule this fair land;
They are the curse of the poor labouring man.

Errol Flynn

Words and music: Michael Raven

Charmer that you are, sitting on your high hill,
If the vodka doesn't get you then the women will.
Robin Hood and Captain Blood all rolled into one,
But one day the sun arose to find you gone.

"Where are you going to, I ask you, pray ?"
Long hot night, long hot day.
"I'm sailing on far beyond the bar,
Sailing through the night to catch a falling star."

"Goodbye Gauguin, hello south of France,
We'll lead those money men a merry dance."
Don't look now, but he's coming for me,
Silver sword a-hanging at his knee.

Bar room brawls and the ladies so fair,
Living for the moment and never a care.
Still he sails on his Southern Sea,
Swinging in his hammock and he's
    laughing at me.

Head in your hands, in your dying days,
Now they're admiring of your wicked ways.
The Sun Also Rises, Too Much Too Soon,
But the dark clouds are racing with the
    blood red moon.

Hampton Lullaby

Words and music: Michael Raven

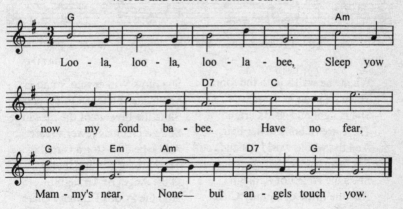

Loo - la, loo - la, loo - la - bee, Sleep yow
now my fond ba - bee. Have no fear,
Mam - my's near, None— but an - gels touch yow.

Loo-la, Loo-la, Loo-la-bee,
Sleep yow now, my fond babee.
Have no fear, Mammy's near,
None but angels touch yow.

See that 'ouse in yonder row,
That's where all the fairies gow.

See that bannock fayther took,
Caught for yow in Smestow Brook.

Your fayther's workin' late for we,
He'll come home to yow and me.

If you'll go to sleep me son,
Ah'll tek yow in to Hampton town

Angel of Armagh

Words and music: Michael Raven

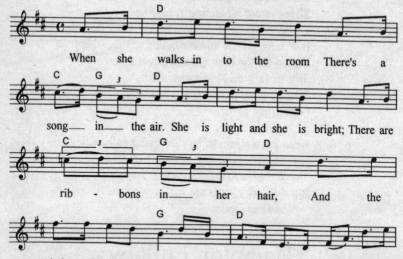

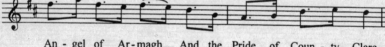

20.7.1999

When she walks in to the room
There's a song in the air.
She is light and she is bright;
There are ribbons in her hair;
And the whole world it stands still
For there's none that can compare.
She's the Angel of Armagh
And the Pride of County Clare.

She turns Winter into Summer;
She makes hope out of despair.
She's the flowers of the meadow;
She's a precious jewel so rare,
And when the storm is raging
The harbour waiting there,
Is the Angel of Armagh
And the Pride of County Clare.

The angel is a
Celtic Queen
of Peace.
The house on
a hill is the
parliament of
a United Ireland.

Oh I will build for you
A house high on the hill
Where servants you shall have
To do with as you will;
And when the sword is sheathed
They'll all say: "We do declare
She's the Angel of Armagh
And the Pride of County Clare."

Hednesford Town

Words and music: Michael Raven

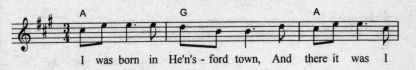

I was born in He'ns-ford town, And there it was I

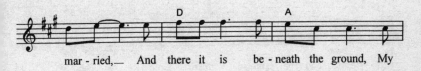

mar-ried,— And there it is be-neath the ground, My

dar-lin' son has tar - ried.

I was born in He'n'sford town,
And there it was I married,
And there it is beneath the ground,
My darlin' son has tarried.

You might scorn the price of coal,
And chide the men who mine it,
But every black and shining piece
Has blood and grief writ on it.

Johnny lad I thinks on you,
And thinks on you right dearly,
Through Summer's sun and Winter's rain,
Like the wind that shakes the barley.

I was born in He'n'sford town,
And there it was I married,
And there it is beneath the ground,
My darlin' son has tarried.

The tune is in the Phrygian mode

Song of the Fox

Words and music: Michael Raven

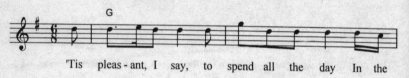

'Tis pleas - ant, I say, to spend all the day In the

fields— and for - ests so green.— Bold Rey - ard and I to -

geth - er would lie, And jol - ly good times we have seen.— But the

lords and their lad - ies all dressed up so fine, With their

hor - ses and wild— hal - loo,—— Came out with their hounds and

hun - ted our grounds, And a - las we came in - to their view.——

'Tis pleasant, I say, to spend all the day
In the fields and forests so green.
Bold Reynard and I together would lie,
And jolly good times we have seen.
But the lords and their ladies all dressed up so fine,
With their horses and wild halloo,
Came out with their hounds and hunted our grounds,
And alas we came into their view.

The mist it rolled up and the mist it rolled down;
They hunted us ten miles or more.
To give me a chance he hung back at The Lance,
And they caught him at Duns-in-the-Moor.
With a spade and a gun they ended his run,
And butchered him there on the spot.
Fine flowers now grow by Highlanders Row,
In the valley that God forgot.

I watched from the hill as they finished the kill;
I saw the green field turn red.
As I turned away I heard the horn play
A tuneless lament for the dead.
Now when winter winds blow in sorrow I go,
To search for his soul on the moor,
And I scream to the moon to let me die soon,
There's nothing left worth living for.

Just three weeks ago the horn it did blow;
Once more the hounds lusted for blood.
They took my young cubs and beat them with clubs,
And trampled them into the mud.
Now when winter winds blow in sorrow I go,
To search for their souls on the moor,
And I scream to the moon to let me die soon;
There's nothing left worth living for.

Shropshire Widow's Lament

Words and music: Michael Raven

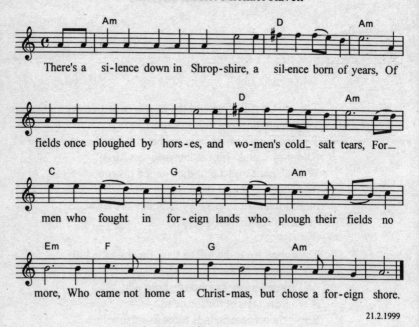

There's a si-lence down in Shrop-shire, a sil-ence born of years, Of fields once ploughed by hors-es, and wo-men's cold_ salt tears, For_ men who fought in for-eign lands who_ plough their fields no more, Who came not home at Christ-mas, but chose a for-eign shore.

21.2.1999

There's a silence down in Shropshire, a silence born of years,
Of fields once ploughed by horses, and womens' cold salt tears,
For men who fought in foreign lands who plough their fields no more,
Who came not home at Christmas, but chose a foreign shore.

Oh, yes, I dance at Christmas, and sing a merry tune,
But when the dancing's done with, and that is all too soon,
I seek a quiet corner to still my aching heart,
And count the growing years that we have been apart.

Oh, yes, I dance at Christmas, and sing a merry tune,
And watch the morn, at break of dawn, farewell the fading moon;
I smile at friends and wish them well, but with my every breath,
I walk the lanes of living that only lead to death.

For grief is now an old friend, and we walk hand in hand,
And every hour he's with me, he makes me understand
That every new day we awake, and see the sun arise,
Closer then the time it come to say our last goodbyes.

Over the Wall

Words and music: Michael Raven

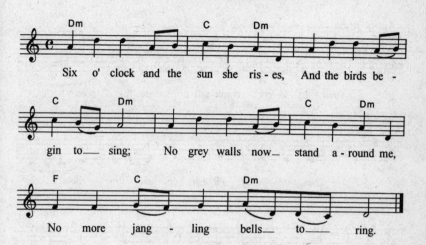

Six o'clock and the sun she rises,
And the birds begin to sing;
No grey walls now stand around me,
No more jangling bells to ring.

On I trudge though the snow is falling
On the forest and the plain;
On I trudge tho' my heart is breaking
Never to see my love again.

Hard it is this life I'm leading,
Cold the winter winds do blow;
Harder yet the life I'm leaving,
Ninety miles or more to go.

Think's I'll take the road to Worcester,
I have friends there I know well;
In the spring perhaps I'll wander,
Wander where I cannot tell.

Yonder comes the sound of music
And the rattle of the big bass drum;
Thinks I might go across and join them,
Dance to the light of the setting sun.

Dancing Lady

Words and music: Michael Raven

Danc - ing la - dy, come tell to me— the score;_____

Danc-ing la-dy, I'll ask you one— time more:_____

When you grow old____ will you be cold,—

Or— have you— a mil - li - on - aire?_____

Dancing lady, come tell to me the score;
Dancing lady, I'll ask you one time more:
When you grow old will you be cold,
Or have you a millionaire?

Slightly faded, slightly jaded flower;
Will you have made it or will your heart turn sour?
Dress yourself gaily, go face them bravely;
Smile your smile once more.

Dancing lady, see the lights shine brightly;
Dancing lady, wearing your heart so lightly;
Dress yourself gaily, go face them bravely:
Smile your smile once more.

The Sands of the Dee

Words and music: Michael Raven

Oh the sands of the_ Dee be-long now to_ me Since_
my love was lost there, so pre-cious was_ she. Like a
li-ly fresh flo-wer that spar-kled so fine; With the
dew of the morn-ing she ev-er is_ mine.

16.10.1998

Oh the sands of the Dee belong now to me
Since my love was lost there, so precious was she.
Like a lily-fresh flower that sparkled so fine;
With the dew of the morning, she ever is mine.

The cattle were lowing, was time they came home,
And then the light darkened, the winds they did moan.
I sent my dear Mary out on to the sand,
But the waters were rising and showed their grim hand.

They found her next morning, the sun on her hair,
My lovely, my lady, my jewel so rare.
Ten years to the day, now, we laid her to rest,
To face the dawn rising from out of the west.

If only cruel fate could change her decree,
I'd be long dead, now, and she'd cry for me.
But she is still with me, her laugh and her smile,
My solace and comfort for many a long mile.

The first verse can also used as a chorus

Lazy Jane

Words and music: Michael Raven

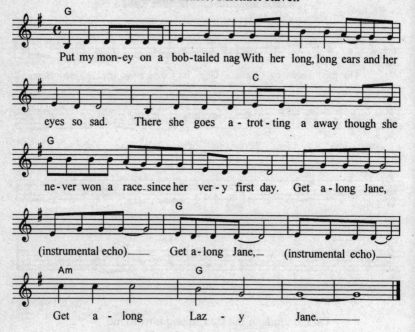

Put my mon-ey on a bob-tailed nag With her long, long ears and her eyes so sad. There she goes a-trot-ting a away though she ne-ver won a race since her ver-y first day. Get a-long Jane, (instrumental echo)____ Get a-long Jane,____ (instrumental echo)____ Get a - long Laz - y Jane.____

Up to the gate and away they go,
Never too fast and never too slow.
Over the fence and would you believe
Down goes the favourite on bended knees?

Round the bend to the water they come
And down goes another in the summer sun.
Seven left now and the pace so fast
And poor little Jane is next to last.

Over the hill up to Rowley End
And two more fall at the Pinewood Bend.
Three in front and she stands a chance
And she smiles at the crowd with a sideways glance.

Furlongs three from the end they are
And the bonny big black has gone too fast.
Down he comes and the chestnut too
And now there's Jane and the Pride of Crewe.

Furlongs two and the bob-tailed nag,
With her long, long ears and her eyes so sad,
Beats the Pride with a burst of speed
That those who saw it said "a marvel indeed".

Now she grazes in a field of green
And in her eyes you'll see a gleam,
And now she moves with a touch of grace
For very few win their very last race.

Rebel Leader's Lament

Words and music: Michael Raven

Now, it is all done.
We are alone, our race is run.
"The night is black, but the sun will rise,
Do not look back," the song bird cries.

My good sword is sharp;
My praises sung by lute and harp.
My heart is true, my arm is strong.
But whispered words ask: "For how long?"

Home, I must head home.
Across these hills too long I've roamed.
At the eagle's nest I'll lay me down.
The weeping moon my funeral gown.

Johnny Jones

Words and music: Michael Raven

The judge he sat in his robes of red,
Looked at me and then he said:
"Johnny lad you're as good as dead
For they'll hang you in the morning."

Hi! Johnny Jones now the wind blows high,
Hi! Johnny Jones now don't be shy,
We'll be there to see you die,
At the hanging in the morning.

Then up jumped screws in their coats so black,
Handcuffed me and took me back;
Hear the trains go clickety clack
To the hanging in the morning.

Rattle of cups on the doors all night,
Rattle of the trains' "Now that ain't right";
Sun comes up and it's broad daylight,
And the chapel bell's a-ringing.

Ten o'clock and the preacher sings;
Ten o'clock and the Governor grins;
Ten o'clock and Johnny swings,
At the hanging in the morning.

Midnight in the City

Words and music: Michael Raven

The sequence A Bm C#m Bm is played over an A bass and E treble pedal notes

Mid-night in the ci-ty,— Flash-ing lights so pret-ty,— Got no one got no-where to go, Is-n't that a pi-ty?— And it has been so long, And it has been so— long, Since I saw you,——————— My— friend you.

Tired and I'm hungry,
But one thought comes to me,
Surely I am not alone,
In this midnight city.

Help me if you can;
Please lend a helping hand,
You're more than all the world to me,
Try to understand.

Flowers in Her Hair

Words and music: Michael Raven

It's si-lent on— the streets to-night, Frost in the air and the moon shines bright,— Day is done and I am home-ward bound.

Smiled to my-self as I thought of him, Some you lose and some you win;— Here's a los-er wait-ing to be found.

John - ny lad where are you now? If on - ly you'd come home.

Be you near or far a-way, Please just write or 'phone.—

Talk to me in the eve - ning light, Noth - ing to say, well that's al - right,— All I want is you and your com-pa - ny.

It's silent on the streets tonight,
Frost in the air and the moon shines bright,
Day is done and I am homeward bound.
Smiled to myself as I thought of him,
Some you lose and some you win;
Here's a loser waiting to be found.

Johnny lad, where are you now?
If only you'd come home.
Be you near or far away,
Please just write or 'phone.
Talk to me in the evening light,
Nothing to say, well, that's all right,
All I want is you and your company.

Oh! Lady Luck never looked on me;
Had a little girl and now she's three,
God knows how we both have got this far.
"Count your blessings" the social said,
Well, I did, I'd be better off dead;
I really, really can't take any more.

Turned on the gas and the world went away;
Flowers in her hair.
Sun comes up, yet another day,
Too late now to care.
Talk to me in the evening light,
Nothing to say, well that's all right.
All I want is you and your company.

Mirror of My Mind

Words and music: Michael Raven

A flash of your eyes be-guil-ing me with sor-row. In your smile a lone-ly sea-bird_ cries; Des-ert winds and danc-ing dream-ers know it; On-ly a fool could be so_ blind; You are the mir-ror of my mind.

CIRCA 1968

A flash of your eyes beguiling me with sorrow.
In your smile a lonely seabird cries;
Desert winds and dancing dreamers know it;
Only a fool could be so blind;
You are the mirror of my mind.

I have seen the sun to shiver silent,
Steal a glance and turn so sad away;
His moon and stars no longer can enchant him;
No fire can more brightly shine.
You are the mirror of my mind.

My soul will not content with reason;
Snakes and giants cackle in my brain.
What if she is gone tomorrow?
Tomorrow I shall wake and find:
You are not the mirror of my mind?

Ruth Ellis

Words and music: Michael Raven

Ruth Ellis is my name, tomorrow I die,
And shooting my true love, I don't deny,
For he did betray me and brought me to shame;
Still no sound is sweeter than the sound of his name.

Chorus:
So bury me here, love, 'neath the old willow tree,
And let the green grass grow, grow over me,
And you must not weep, love, and you must not cry,
Tomorrow they hang me, tomorrow I die.

I came home one evening, came by the back way,
And there was my true love, with another he lay;
My poor heart was broken, my pistol I drew,
With tears overflowing my true love I slew.

Bentley Canal

Words and music: Michael Raven

Dream - ing, dream - ing of the days gone by; Fad-ing, fad - ing fast I'm dy - ing. Once my wa - ters sang and touched the sky. Now I am sad and wea— ry, Now the boats are gone,— No one ev - en knows my name.

Dreaming, dreaming of the days gone by;
Fading, fading fast I'm dying.
Once my waters sang and touched the sky.

Chorus:
Now I'm sad and weary,
Now the boats are gone,
No one even knows my name.

Sailing, sailing on a midnight shroud;
Laughing, laughing though I'm crying.
When the foundry boats came I was proud.

Smiling, smiling as the day grows dim;
Lying, sighing though I'm crying.
Once I told myself that I could win.

New Year

Words and music: Michael Raven

The gen - tle sighs of lute and ly - re

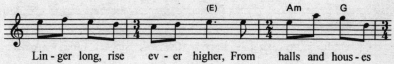

Lin - ger long, rise ev - er higher, From halls and hous - es

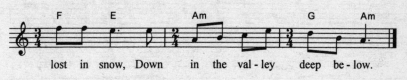

lost in snow, Down in the val - ley deep be - low.

8.2.1999

The gentle sighs of lute and lyre
Linger long, rise ever higher,
From halls and houses lost in snow,
Down in the valley deep below.

The earth and sky are in accord;
The mighty lord lays down his sword;
The fox bays down the moon at night,
And with the dawn all is quite right.

The church bells' chimes are muffled now,
And berries red weigh down the bough.
The robin sings in praise of God,
And shivering pines approval nod.

The fire crackles in the grate;
The clock ticks down our certain fate;
An old dog yawns and flicks his ear,
To welcome in this bright New Year.

This song can also be accompanied
with a drone on the note A (or A and E)

Mountain Tree

Words and music: Michael Raven

Oh come and see my moun - tain tree, And watch my swal - lows fly - ing free, And cheer the hare come hun - ted home, And see the moon rise all a - lone.

20.7.1999

Oh come and see my mountain tree,
And watch my swallows flying free,
And cheer the hare come hunted home,
And see the moon rise all alone.

The ragged line of noble pine;
The lambs at play come Summertime;
The high-born hills with heads held proud:
The evening mist their wedding shroud.

And see the storm and lightning flash;
These bold night-riders cut a dash
And madly dance with wind and rain
'Till anger slows to mere disdain.

Oh come and see the wind in corn;
The lark rise up, sing in the morn;
The rivers dream, the cattle graze,
And you will stay all of your days.

Little White Donkey

Words and music: Michael Raven
The rhythm is of the South American rhumba: 123,123,12

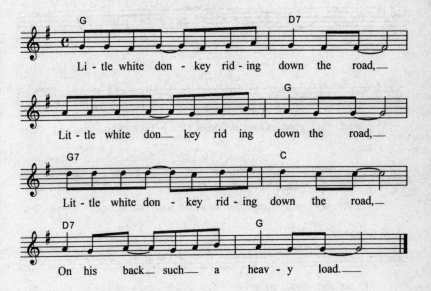

Li - tle white don - key rid - ing down the road,—

Lit - tle white don— key rid ing down the road,—

Lit - tle white don - key rid - ing down the road,—

On his back— such— a heav - y load.—

Little white donkey riding down the road,
Little white donkey riding down the road,
Little white donkey riding down the road,
On his back such a heavy load.

Chorus:
Ay, ay, ay, such a heavy load, (x3)
Little white donkey riding down the road.

As they ride his master sing a song,
"Come little donkey it won't be long."

Over the hills and far away,
On that long hot Summer's day.

High upon the cross he'll hang,
He's not a king, not even a man.

He is the Christ and for us died,
He is the Christ we crucified.

Great Train Robbery

Words and music: Michael Raven

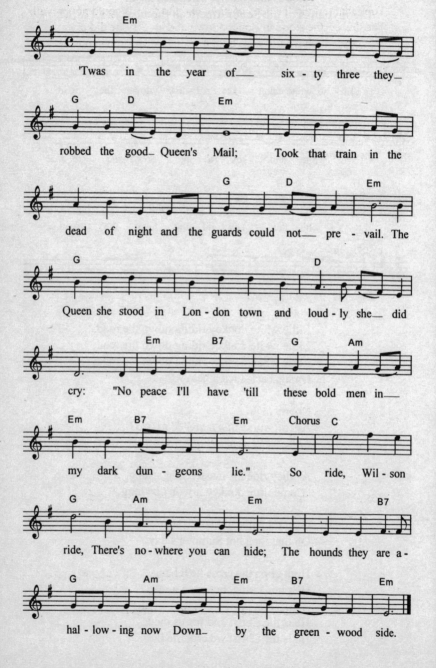

'Twas in the year of—— six - ty three they——
robbed the good— Queen's Mail; Took that train in the
dead of night and the guards could not— pre - vail. The
Queen she stood in Lon - don town and loud - ly she— did
cry: "No peace I'll have 'till these bold men in——
my dark dun - geons lie." So ride, Wil - son
ride, There's no - where you can hide; The hounds they are a-
hal - low - ing now Down— by the green - wood side.

'Twas in the year of sixty-three they robbed the good Queen's mail;
Took that train in the dead of night and the guards could not prevail.
The Queen she stood in London town and loudly she did cry:
"No peace I'll have till these bold men in my dark dungeons lie."

A wealthy man was Wilson now, likewise his bold comrades,
And into hiding he did go, but shortly was betrayed.
The law they came and he was tried and he got thirty years,
And now the Queen could lay her head and dry her cold salt tears.

Winson Green it is a place of long forgotten souls,
A curse upon fair Birmingham, as you must surely know;
But Wilson had bright shining gold and with it bribed a screw;
One stormy night he took flight with the hounds all in full view.

Chorus:
So ride, Wilson, ride,
There's nowhere you can hide;
The hounds they are a-hallowing now
Down by the greenwood side.

He took the road to sunny France where lords and ladies dwell,
And with his wife did lead a life of luxury full well;
Dancing in the dim cafes and drinking sweet champagne,
But to the sun the hounds did run, such is the price of fame.

Chorus

Finally to Canada bold Wilson did arrive,
And in that land of ice and snow he found a place to hide.
He took a house and called his wife and they did settle down;
But while he slept in the night there crept the good Queen's
    stealthy hounds.

Chorus

For two short years he lived content and then there came the day
Mounties stood his house about, and careful watch kept they.
Straight from England there arrived two servants of the Queen,
And so once more she locked the door of Mercy and 'The Green'.

The Drover's Song

Words: Padraic Colum and Michael Raven;
music: Michael Raven

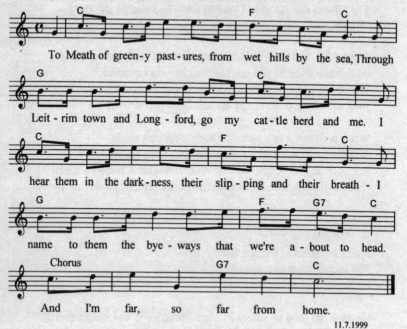

To Meath of green-y past-ures, from wet hills by the sea, Through Leit-rim town and Long-ford, go my cat-tle herd and me. I hear them in the dark-ness, their slip-ping and their breath - I name to them the bye-ways that we're a-bout to head.

Chorus
And I'm far, so far from home.

11.7.1999

To Meath of greeny pastures, from wet hills by the sea,
Through Leitrim town and Longford, go my cattle herd and me.
I hear them in the darkness, their slipping and their breath -
I name to them the bye-ways that we're about to head.

The wet and winding roads, and brown bogs with black water;
And my thoughts are on white ships and the King of Spain's daughter.
Oh! farmer strong, oh farmer! you can spend well at the fair;
But then must turn your face and go, your crops are needing care.

The acrid smell of cattle, the wet wind in the morn;
And the proud and undug earth that ne'er was broke for corn;
The coloured crowds at fair-time, the herds loosened and blind,
Loud words and darkened faces and the wild blood behind.

There's many a long night as I've slept in the rain,
Beneath a hedge or in a stack until the morning came.
With morning's glory I arise, the dew all on the grass:
There's many a long mile to go before we reach the pass.

The Maid and the Morrismen

Words and music: Michael Raven

As I walked out one morn in May,
Hey ho, come dilly come day, I met four morrismen
on the way; Hey ho, come dilly come day. I
met four morrismen on the way, Said one: "Fair maid please
come and play," And we will sing a roun - de - lay,
Hey ho, come dilly come day.

11.7.1999

As I walked out one morn in May,
Hey ho, come dilly come day,
I met four morrismen on the way;
Hey ho, come dilly come day.
I met four morrismen on the way,
Said one: "Fair maid please come
    and play,"
And we will sing a roundelay.
Hey ho, come dilly come day.

Says I to him: "What is your trade?"
Says he: "I am a miller, dear maid."
So, says I: "One night with me
Your grindstone it will ground
    down be."

The next I ask he is quite old;
Says he: "I am soldier bold,"
So, says I: "One night with me
Your sword I warrant will rusted be."

The next I ask is quite comely;
Says he: "I am a ploughman free,
So, says I: "One night with me
Your ploughshare will quite
    blunted be."

The last I ask is quite jolly;
"I am a sperm whaler just home
    from sea,
Says I: "Good sir I beg of thee
When shall we two married be?"

Che Guevara

Words and music: Michael Raven

Sing Che—— Gue - var - a,——— — for Che he's a - way——— To the for - ests and moun - tains,——— at the dawn of the day.———

Chorus:
Sing Che Guevara, for Che he's away
To the forests and mountains, at the dawn of the day.
Sing Che guevara, for Che he's away,
To the forests and mountains, at the dawn of the day.

There's fire on the mountains, there's fire on the hills;
There's fire in the valleys, no tyrant can still;
And though you may lie there, your body all bones,
The sun also rises, they day always dawns.

No drum to beat lowly, no bugles to ring;
No coffin to carry, no song for to sing;
No priest for to praise you, no friends for to mourn,
But the sun also rises, the day always dawns.

White Rose

Words and music: Michael Raven
The chorus comes after each pair of verses

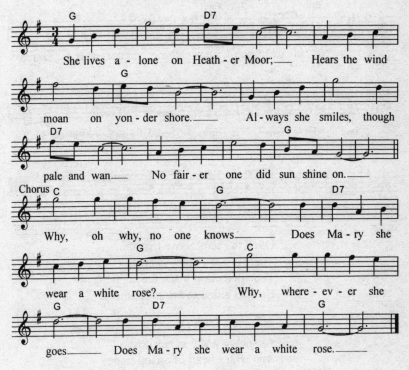

She lives alone on Heather Moor;
Hears the wind moan on yonder
  shore.
Always she smiles, though pale
  and wan;
No fairer one did sun shine on.

Black is her hair with ribbons tied.
"Weary am I" this fair maid sighed.
Always a rose is in her hair,
When Mary goes to Swansea Fair.

Far, far away in Tahiti
There is a bar beside the sea.
Brown girls they dance and sing
  a song;
Sailors they drink there all
  night long.

High on a hill, beyond the town,
Lies a low mound above the Sound.
Here shining bright in darkest night
A blood red rose and one of white.

On Summer nights she sits at
  home
Staring to sea and all alone.
As the sun sinks she sees him
  walk
Up from the shore and then they
  talk.

So many things there are to say
For he has been so long away,
But come the dark he turns and
  goes,
Giving to her his last white rose.

The White Gloves

Words: Michael Raven; music: Welsh traditional

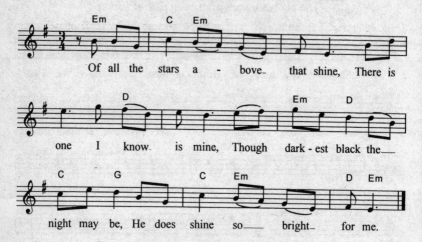

Of all the stars above that shine,
There is one I know is mine,
Though darkest black the night may be,
He does shine so bright for me.

The judge he hid his snow white gloves,
As snowy white as any dove,
And with a heart of prison stone
Took a life no man should own.

I wish I had a castle tall,
A golden calf, a barren stall,
And I would sing a lullaby,
I care not if I live or die.

There is a lake of deep despair,
And swans of mercy they sleep there.
No cannon's roar nor young girl's scream
Can wake them from their blissful dream.

*It was the custom for a judge to wear
white gloves on the last day of an Assize
court at which the death penalty
had not been given.*

Stafford Pageant Song

Words: Michael Raven; music: Staines Morris

Come you Lords and Ladies fair,
Dress you gay, tie up your hair,
For today we'll merry, merry be
At Stafford's Fair and Pageantry.

Then to the Fair haste ye away
For 'tis now our Pageant Day.

Jousting knights in armour bright
Fight and die for your delight;
Ladies of such beauty there
As never were seen at a county Fair.

Enter now the famed Sealed Knot
With cannons roar and musket shot;
One hundred men or more there be
To prove King Charles' victory.

Acrobats and jugglers too,
Show their tricks both old and new;
Shows to please you one and all;
Young and old they will enthral.

Here's a toast to the Pageant Queen;
She brings good luck and the leaves so green.
God bless her and everyone;
Summer is a-come and winter is gone.

Valley of Dreams

Words: Michael Raven; music: Scottish traditional

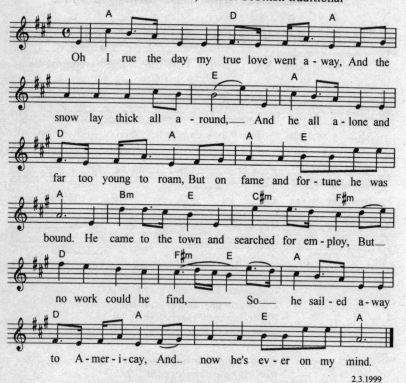

2.3.1999

Oh I rue the day my true love went away,
And the snow lay thick all around,
And he all alone and far too young to roam,
But on fame and fortune he was bound.
He came to the town and searched for employ,
But no work could he find,
So he sailed away to Americay,
And now he's ever on my mind.

I hope and I pray that he'll come home one day,
And to the church we both will go,
And the church bells will ring, and my poor heart will sing,
For I love my handsome Johnny so.
And when we are wed, and all our vows are said,
We'll build us a cottage by the stream,
And there'll we'll live and die, and forever lie,
In the valley of a lonely girl's dream.

Fair Land

Words: Michael Raven; music: traditional / Michael Raven

'Tis— pleas-ant I say to spend all the day On the riv-er 'till eve-ning do come,— When the sun it goes down and the on-ly sweet sound Are the wat-ers that gen-tly do run.— Oh— there nev-er was such a

Chorus

fair_____ land; Oh there nev-er was nor can be. So_____ when I do die I beg let me lie In the—fair earth of old— Eng-land._____

CIRCA 1980

Oh the robin and rose, the cold wind that blows,
The rain that falls high on the lea;
The lark in the morn, the sheep to be shorn,
The corn lying fallow in field.

Oh the verdant green vale, the dark rolling dale,
The mist rolling in from the sea;
The birds of the air, there's none can compare
With the fair land of England for me.

Oh the sailor at sea he never can be
Afraid of the wild ocean's roar,
For he's of the blood that battled and stood
And kept the foe from our fair shore.

Gabriel's Hounds

Words: Michael Raven; music: English traditional

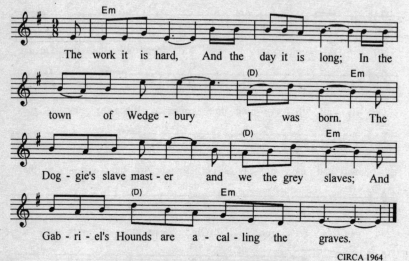

CIRCA 1964

The Buttie he robs, the Tommy likewise;
In the town of Wedgebury I was born,
There's little but hardship, the pick and the mine;
And Gabriel's Hounds are giving the sign.

It's Saturday night at the Cockfighter's Arms;
In the town of Wedgebury I was born.
I'll give a robin for a cock any day;
And Gabriel's Hounds are having their say.

Sunday's a holiday and Monday likewise;
Tuesday you means to but cannot arise;
Wednesday you wants to and Thursday you tries;
Friday and Saturday the Whistler he he cries.

In the Thirty-Foot Coal I spent all my days.
If you ask the Buttie he'll give you a raise;
Give you more silver but truck it away;
For Gabriel's Hounds will have their way.

The nailors and cutlers lead very hard lives;
They likened to Lazarus and we unto Dives,
But look at the Maloch and you'll understand,
It's Gabriel's Hounds rule over this land.

Little Birds of the Mountain

Words: Michael Raven; music: Welsh traditional

"Oh, come to me my night-in-gale, And bring the lark of Sum-mer, And all the small birds of the hill, And go to my true lov-er.

8.6.1998

"For she is weak and to her bed;
Go take to her this letter,
No precious jewel have I to give.
Just say I'll not forget her."

And all that day and all that night,
They flew their journey long,
O'er hill and dale and valleys wide,
And for her sang their song.

"Oh, little birds, you pretty birds,
You small birds of the mountain,
Why do you sing so sweet for me,
Like sunlight on the fountain."

"Oh, we are come to wish you well,
Your true love lies in sorrow,
And these white gloves a gift he sends,
And prays good health will follow."

She smiled a smile, both thin and wan,
A tear fell from her eye.
"Alas, by Summer's end I go,
In cold, cold earth to lie.

"But tell him gentle, tell him kind,
That to my God I go.
I rest in peace, he must not grieve,
And that I love him so."

Ballad of Jonathan Wild

Words: Michael Raven; music: English traditional

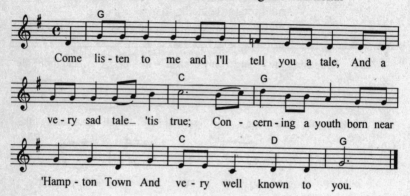

Come listen to me and I'll tell you a tale, And a very sad tale 'tis true; Concerning a youth born near 'Hampton Town And very well known to you.

Come listen to me and I'll tell you a tale,
And a very sad tale 'tis true;
Concerning a youth born near 'Hampton Town
And very well known to you.

He was bound to trade in fair Brummagem,
And bound to trade was he;
He took him a wife, the joy of his life,
And a boy child soon bore she.

Now Jonathan Wild was a gay young man,
And a gay young man was he;
But the star of the east it burned his eye,
And to London he did flee.

He ran and he ran and he ran all night;
He ran and he ran all day
Until he came to the coal-black Thames,
A while there for to stay.

He bought him a coat of the best bright blue
And shirts of silk so rare;
And boots of leather from the lands of Spain,
And his horse was a snow white mare.

But into prison then he was flung
For debts he could not pay;
And there he met with a wicked woman,
And to him these words she did say:

"Oh come along with me , my love,
And through the fields so green,
And we will rob all on the highway
Our fortunes to redeem."

But John he had a very clever plan
As cunning as it was bold;
So he called all the thieves and gay vagabonds,
His scheme to them he told.

"Now all of you who rob by night
And drink good ale by day,
Bring unto me all that you take
And you shall not dismay.

"For I will stand as a gentleman,
And a taker of fine thieves,
And at a cost of a quarter share
Their goods I shall retrieve."

Then a singing man and a fiddler bold
Played a lively tune,
And so they danced, oh how they danced
To the dying of the moon.

Wild he bought him a tall fine ship,
As fair as sailed the sea,
To take his gold and bright diamonds
To France and Germany.

But she was betrayed and John likewise,
His time it was well nigh;
And tried he was at the Old Bailey,
And there condemned to die.

To Tyburn Hill in the gallows cart,
No ear to hear his plea;
And he drank the drink that Shepherd left,
And swung from the gallows tree.

Wyrley Broom

Words: Michael Raven; music: traditional adapted by Michael Raven

When Wyr-ley broom's in blos-som It makes my heart to grieve, For— then it was they took her With blood up-on her sleeve. She was my own true moth-er and reared me ten-der-ly, And of-ten I re-mem-ber the words she said to me: "Oh, do not weep my dar-ling, Your fath-er knows the lie: 'Twas Ward and Rich-ards killed him, And for them I must die."

When Wyrley Broom's in blossom
It makes my heart to grieve,
For then it was they took her
With blood upon her sleeve.
She was my own true mother
And reared me tenderly
And often I remember
The words she said to me:
"Oh do not weep my darling,
Your father knows the lie:
'Twas Ward and Richards killed him,
And for them I must die."

I took my father's rifle,
And rode into the town,
And there was Richards drinking,
Making a merry sound.
I followed him that evening,
And God sent me a gale;
I buried him in moonlight,
And loud the winds did wail.
No cross was there to mark his grave,
No words of blessing read,
And Wyrley Broom in blossom,
A pillow for his head.

I took my mother's pistol,
And rode up to the farm,
Past the cattle grazing,
And past the broken barn.
There stood Ward and smiling,
He bid me "Well-a-day,"
And there his blood fell heavy,
As in the corn he lay.
No sound was there but summer,
And silent fields around,
With Wyrley Broom in blossom,
My vengeance I had found.

I went up to the churchyard,
To where my father lay,
And told him to lie easy,
His debts in full I'd paid.
To fell the
Rowan
tree is to
commit
suicide
But he rose up in anger
And cursed my very name:
"Like her, you are a butcher,
And bitter is my shame.
It was your mother killed me;
A murderer are thee."
With Wyrley Broom in blossom,
I felled the Rowan tree.

Tanunda Road

Words: Michael Raven; music: traditional adapted by Michael Raven

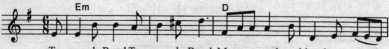

Ta - nun-da Road, Ta - nun-da Road, Ma-ny a good seed has been sowed,

Ma - ny a gamb-ler's shot his load, Down in South Aus tra - li - a.

Crea-tures paint - ed par-rot green, Float-ing in— this steam - ing dream;

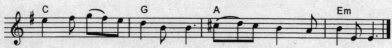

Fields of char - don - ay I've seen, Down— in South Aus - tra-li - a.

Tanunda Road, Tanunda Road,
Many a good seed has been sowed,
Many a gambler's shot his load,
Down in South Australia.
Creatures painted parrot green,
Floating in this steaming dream;
Fields of chardonay I've seen,
Down in South Australia.

Memories of Errol Flynn,
Lusty ladies quick to sin,
Play the game but never win,
Down in South Australia.
I remember Tico's Bar,
Nights beneath his Southern Star,
Robbed me blind but there you are,
Down in South Australia.

Hoochie Coochie bleary-eyed,
"Here my man ," this brown maid sighed,
Oh my God I nearly died,
Down in South Australia.
Tin sheds stand in scorched array,
They sweat all night; they sweat all day.
God came once but didn't stay,
Down in South Australia.

John Collins

Words: Michael Raven; music: traditional, adapted by Michael Raven

The sergeant he said: "You're John Collins, I
know by your face you're my man, So make your farewells and be
hasty, For soon you'll be on the stone gang."

The sergeant he said: "You're John Collins,
I know by your face you're my man,
So make your farewells and be hasty,
For soon you'll be on the stone gang."

They tried me by judge and by jury,
By twelve good men and true,
But the judge he was Justice Argyle, Sir,
So I got twelve years 'stead of two.

To the Scrubs I was sent the next morning,
'Twas there that I fought with a screw,
For he called me the scum of the earth, Sir,
Now what was a poor man to do?

To the hospital he was straight taken,
On Monday they took me away;
On Thursday he died in the morning,
A-calling my name, so they say.

I offer no plea for a pardon,
I offer no prayers for his soul,
For that Judge Argyle and his screws, Sir,
Must tempt even God to be cruel.

So come you good people and listen,
Listen while I say unto you:
There's justice for judges and juries,
But there's little justice for you.

Morgan the Hammer

Words: Michael Raven; music: traditional, adapted by Michael Raven

28.9.1998

I am Morgan, I the Hammer,
I strike fire and flames for Him.
Every waking hour I labour
For my place in Heaven to win.

Place in Heaven,
Place in Heaven,
For my place in Heaven to win,
In Heaven to win.

Out there in the mighty mountains,
Out there in the wind and snow,
Old men cry out for forgiveness;
Widows weep and and salt tears
    flow.

Weep and salt tears,
Weep and salt tears,
Widows weep and salt tears flow,
And salt tears flow.

Hear the iron, she cries in
    anguish:
Every blow means one sin less.
Hear the hiss as water kiss her,
Tempered in his sweet caress.

In his sweet,
In his sweet,
Tempered in His sweet caress,
His sweet caress.

I am Morgan of the Hammer,
In my heart just one desire:
That my God smile down upon
    me;
For my Lord I'm striking fire.

Lord I'm striking,
Lord I'm striking,
For my Lord I'm striking fire,
I'm striking fire.

Sons of Glyndwr

Words; Michael Raven; music: traditional Welsh funeral hymn

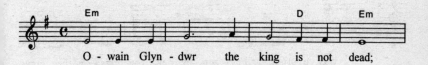

O - wain Glyn - dwr the king is not dead;

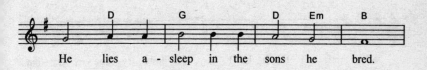

He lies a - sleep in the sons he bred.

Ring, bu - gles ring, your ral - ly - ing cry:

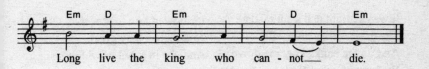

Long live the king who can - not___ die.

Owain Glyndwr the king is not dead;
He lies asleep in the sons he bred.
Ring, bugles ring, your rallying cry:
Long live the king who cannot die.

Murmering streams and whispering trees
Bid you awake and heed their pleas:
Leave you the hills, the mine and the fire;
Drive you the foe from every shire.

Mourn for your dead, their blood it ran red;
Speak you the word long gone unsaid.
Ring, bugles ring, your rallying cry:
Long live the king who cannot die.

Lone Pine

Words: Michael Raven; music: English traditional

It was a bright and a sun-ny day, The gras-ses they grew

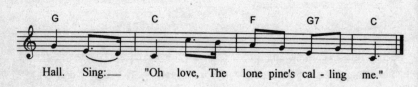

tall, And on the banks I lay me down By bon-ny Gar-but

Hall. Sing:— "Oh love, The lone pine's cal-ling me."

It was a bright and a sunny day,
The grasses they grew tall,
And on the banks I lay me down
By bonny Garbut Hall.

Chorus:
Sing: "Oh love, the lone pine's
Calling me."

Then in the wood I saw a man
As dark as night he be,
And with him walked a coal-black
    dog,
A sadly sight to see.

For his poor head it hung so low,
Tears from his eyes did flow,
And his hound its tail did hang
So very, very low.

I followed him to the River Clun,
And there a lady greet,
And she in a veil of widow's silk,
So comely and so neat.

He smiled at her, she smiled at him,
They curtseyed and they bowed,
Linked arms and slowly walked,
And the willows cried out loud.

They walked into the river,
A cloud it crossed the sun,
And they were gone forever,
A new life was begun.

But the hound as black as midnight,
He howled and he moaned,
And wanders that dark valley,
And wanders all alone.

Song for Diana

Words: Michael Raven; music: traditional, adapted Michael Raven

Now the waters they run gentle,
And the willows mind the way,
And like the winds of winter shed a tear.
They guard her in the morning,
And through each fading day,
On an island they call England, far away.

And the flowers they are smiling.
In every run and rill;
The wild birds they are mourning on the hill.
And shire bells are ringing:
'From flesh and blood to clay',
On an island they call England, far away.

And now the hunt is over,
And mortal maid lies dead,
And priests are done with praying, lessons read,
The grey skies now awaken
To a new and shining day,
On an island they call England, far away.

King Louis

Words: Michael Raven; music: traditional

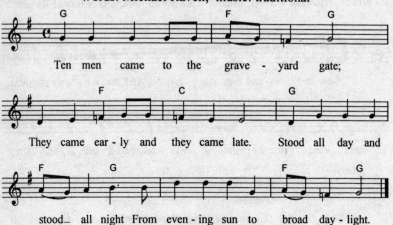

Ten men came to the grave - yard gate;
They came ear - ly and they came late. Stood all day and
stood_ all night From even - ing sun to broad day - light.

Ten men came to the graveyard gate;
They came early and they came late.
Stood all day and stood all night
From evening sun to broad daylight.

One was old and one was grey;
One came from lands far away.
One was young and one was tall
And all came home to bear the pall.

Fill up the cup and fill the can;
Drink a toast to the life of a man.
Drink a toast to the living dead,
And grind their bones for want of bread.

Bread for the weak and bread for the poor;
We'll come no more unto your door.
God's in heaven and hell's on fire;
Hear the bells ring shire to shire.

Captains, Clerks and all of State
And all you who trade in hate,
Count your coins and sleep no more;
There's no use to bar your door.

Oh riddle me this and riddle me that,
What is round and fat as a cat?
The King as he sits upon his throne
And as he sits he sits alone.

Now the plague has done its deed;
Men lie dead in every field.
Birds of the air are singing clear,
But their time is dreadful near.

Oh riddle me this and riddle me that,
What is prettier than a cat?
The Queen as she sleeps on her bed,
And sleeps the sleep of the living dead.

Now the people march along,
And as they march they sing this song:
We were weak but now are strong
As the road we march along.

The gay Cavalier to the war has gone;
He rode off with his horse and gun.
He rode off to a foreign shore
And he will return no more.

He was laid by an English shot;
Now he lies where he should not.
Where the sun it burns the plain,
He lies dead in the lands of Spain.

Farewell to Llangyfelach

Words: Michael Raven, translated from the Welsh;
music: Welsh traditional

Oh fare thee well, my—— coun-try dear, And
all young girls both— far and near, For I must know if
I can find A land more pleas-ing—— to my mind.

6.6.1998

Then a letter came upon one day,
That I must leave and sail away,
That I must serve Her Majesty,
And serve upon the cold salt sea.

In sore distress I left my home,
And made my way to Cowbridge Town,
And there I found great fun and sport,
And 'listed with the Duke of York.

Then in some alehouse I did see
The gold and silver flowing free.
The fifes and drums played rousing tunes,
And so I joined the Light Dragoons.

And girls there were from every town,
And some were ladies of renown.
We sang and drank the night away,
Until we'd spent all of our pay.

And then to London we did go,
To train with swords and make a show
With gun and powder and lead shot;
Our friends at home we near forgot.

So farewell father and mother dear,
Your son is gone and lost I fear.
It is the Queen I now obey,
And will until my dying day.

Tomorrow morn we sail for France,
To fight the foe and make them dance,
And I will see if their country
Compares with mine by fair degree.

If any ask who sang this song
Tell them a maid who waited long,
A maid now lost in grief and pain,
And prays her love return again.

Unspoken Words

Michael Raven

If all the world were mine to own
I'd give her everything.
With all the birds at my command
All day for her they'd sing.

Only gentle rains would fall
And gentle breezes blow.
The moon would guard her whilst she slept,
And all the world would know:

That every word was ever said
Must be a whispered prayer,
And every sentence ever read,
An ode to her so fair.

But she as yet knows none of this -
No prayers, no songs, no birds -
For when my love beside me stands
I am quite lost for words.

11.7.1999

Restless Road

Words: Michael Raven; music: traditional

The restless road is calling me, I've wandered all my life.
My songs are all that I do own and I'll be no man's wife.
My father hoped that I would be a girl of some renown,
But now I'm just a singer in a café in the town.

And you can hear me singing any night or any day,
To people who never hear a word, a word of what I say.
My blanket at night is the starlit sky, and I never ask for why,
The restless road does own my soul and will until I die.

Still, I can have no regrets and no one can I blame;
Another place, another face, another town or name.
I'll wander through this weary world, to where I do not know,
And put my trust in fortune, though fortune be my foe.

My Bonny Lads Away

Words: Michael Raven; music: English traditional,
adapted by Michael Raven

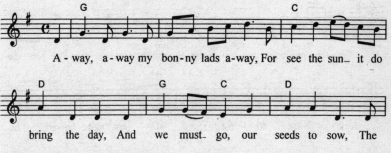

A - way, a - way my bon-ny lads a-way, For see the sun_ it do

bring the day, And we must_ go, our seeds to sow, The

fields to_mow of_ Eng - land's foe, My bon - ny lads a - way.

Away, away my bonny lads away,
For see the sun it do bring the day,
And we must go, our seeds to sow,
The fields to mow of England's foe,
My bonny lads away.

Then to the Somme in the fields of France,
'Twas there we made the Huns to dance.
With Haig in his bed we counted our dead,
And praises said in a hail of lead,
All on the fields of France.

The trenches we dug for many were a grave,
With spade in hand you were nothing but a slave.
So over the top, just another crop,
Ready for the chop, and that's your lot,
In the land of the free and brave.

Now here's to the ladies we left behind;
Treat them well be not unkind,
For widows weeds mean a heart that bleeds,
And our gallant deeds leave them in need,
Oh fare thee well my love.

Turpin's Farewell to Black Bess

Words: verses Michael Raven, chorus traditional; music:
traditional, from May Bradley of Broseley, Shropshire

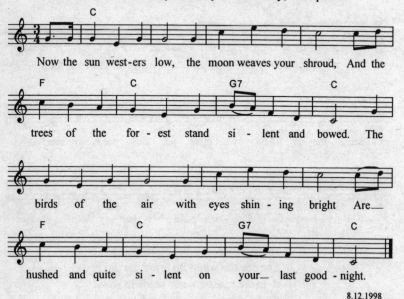

8.12.1998

Now the sun westers low, the moon weaves your shroud,
And the trees of the forest stand silent and bowed.
The birds of the air with eyes shining bright
Are hushed and quite silent on your last goodnight.

Chorus:
Thee shall die my dear friend, and your soul go to rest,
And for kindness I'll shoot thee, my bonny Black Bess.
Ne'er toll bar could stop her, no fear she'd express,
And for kindness I'll shoot thee, my bonny Black Bess.

My heart it is breaking, my tears overflow
To a far better place, Bess, now you have to go.
But it won't be long, friend, till I follow on,
And once more we'll ride to our place in the sun.

So here's to the years we've spent, you and me,
And the miles we have travelled, so far and so free,
You're heart next to mine in the frost and the snow;
With love and in honour this grace I bestow.

Myrtle Tree

Words and music: Michael Raven

The old man stood a - lone as eve came on. The light of day was all but done and gone. "I knew chan - ges would come", said he, "But did they have to take my myr - tle tree?

4.7.1999

The old man stood alone as eve came on.
The light of day was all but done and gone.
"I knew changes would come", said he,
"But did they have to take my myrtle tree?

"Oh I remember well the Summer shade,
The smiles and tears, the games we played
When I was young and fancy free.
Why did they have to take my myrtle tree?

"So, here's to memories; all things must end.
And here's to you again, my dear old friend;
But still I ask:Why should it have to be -
Why did they have to take my myrtle tree?"

Echo

Words: Christina Georgina Rossetti; music Michael Raven

Come to me in the sil - ence of the ni - ght; Come in the speak - ing sil - ence of a dream; Come_ with soft_ round - ed_ cheeks and_ eyes as bright As sun - light on a str - eam; Come back in tears, O mem' ry, hope, love of_ fin - ished_ years.

14.2.1999

Come to me in the silence of the night;
Come in the speaking silence of a dream;
Come with soft rounded cheeks and eyes as bright
As sunlight on a stream;
Come back in tears,
O memory, hope, love of finished years.

O dream how sweet, too sweet, too bitter sweet,
Whose wakening should have been in Paradise,
Where souls brimful of love abide and meet;
Where thirsting longing eyes
Watch the slow door
That opening, letting in, lets out no more.

Yet come to me in dreams that I may live
My very life again though cold in death:
Come back to me in dreams, that I may give
Pulse for pulse, breath for breath;
Speak low, speak lean,
As long ago, my love, as long ago!

A Naked House

Words: Robert Louis Stevenson; music: Michael Raven

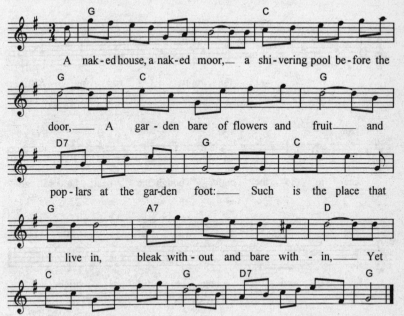

A nak-ed house, a nak-ed moor,— a shi-vering pool be-fore the door,— A gar-den bare of flowers and fruit— and pop-lars at the gar-den foot:— Such is the place that I live in, bleak with-out and bare with-in,— Yet shall your rag-ged moor re-ceive the won-ders of a sum-mer's eve.

10.2.1999

A naked house, a naked moor, a shivering pool before the door,
A garden bare of flowers and fruit and poplars at the garden foot:
Such is the place that I live in, bleak without and bare within,
Yet shall your ragged moor receive the wonders of a summer's eve,

And the cold glories of the dawn, behind your shivering trees
    be drawn;
And when the wind from place to place doth the unmoored cloud-
    galleons chase,
Your garden gloom and gleam again, with leaping sun, with
    glancing rain.
Here shall the wizard moor ascend the heavens, in the crimson end

Of day's declining splendour; here the army of the stars appear.
The neighbour hollows dry or wet, spring shall with tender
    flowers beset;
And oft the morning muser sees larks rising from the broomy lea,
And every fairy wheel and thread of cobweb dew-bediamonded.

So, we'll go no more a-roving

Words: Lord Byron (George Gordon Noel); music: Michael Raven

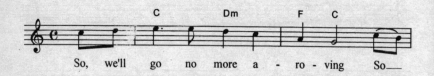

So, we'll go no more a - ro - ving So—

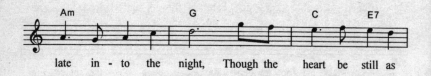

late in - to the night, Though the heart be still as

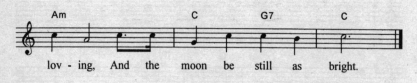

lov - ing, And the moon be still as bright.

12.2.1999

So, we'll go no more a-roving
So late into the night,
Though the heart be still as loving,
And the moon be still as bright.

For the sword outwears its sheath,
And the soul wears out the breast,
And the heart must pause to breathe,
And love itself have rest.

Though the night was made for loving,
And the day returns too soon,
Yet we'll go no more a-roving
By the light of the moon.

Malvern Hills

Words: John Drinkwater; music: Michael Raven

11.7.1999

Cool where the clean winds travel among the solemn hills,
We watch the flowing splendour that Summer brews and spills
From Malvern down to Bredon across the mellow plain,
Transfiguring the lowlands of shining leaves and grain.

Above the black pine-shadows we dream beneath the sky,
And watch the far-flung valleys of Severn and of Wye,
And see the white clouds out walking the great blue road that spans
The world from Wales to Cotswold, like ghostly caravans.

From beacon on to beacon, from shire to burning shire
The full day flames triumphant all girt in golden fire,
And here above the meadows fire-garmented and shod,
We find a little haven among the winds of God.

The Fighting Temeraire

Words: Sir Henry Newbolt; music: Michael Raven

It was eight bells ring-ing, For the morn-ing watch was done,. And the

gun-ner's lads were sing-ing As they pol-ished ev-ery gun. It was

eight bells ring-ing, And the gun-ner's lads—were sing-ing,— For the

ship she rode a-swing-ing As they pol-ished ev-ery gun.—Now the

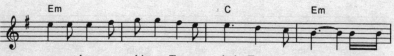

sun-set bree-zes shi-ver, Temer-aire! Tem-er-aire!—And she's

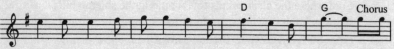

fad-ing down the riv-er, Tem-er-aire! Tem-er-aire!— Now the

sun-set bree-zes shi-ver, And she's fad-ng down the ri-ver,—But in

Eng-land's song for ev-er She's the Fight-ing Tem-er-aire.—

7.2.1999

It was eight bells ringing,
For the morning watch was done,
And the gunner's lads were singing
As they polished every gun.
It was eight bells ringing,
And the gunner's lads were singing,
For the ship she rode a-swinging
As they polished every gun.

Now the sunset breezes shiver,
Temeraire! Temeraire!
And she's fading down the river,
Temeraire! Temeraire!
Now the sunset breezes shiver,
And she's fading down the river,
But in England's song for ever
She's the Fighting Temeraire.

It was noontide ringing,
And the battle just begun,
When the ship her way was winging
As they loaded every gun.
It was noontide ringing,
When the ship her way was winging,
And the gunner's lads were singing
As they loaded every gun.

There's a far bell ringing
At the setting of the sun,
And a phantom voice is singing
Of the great days done.
There's a far bell ringing,
And a phantom voice is singing
Of renown for every clinging
To the great days done.

The Temeraire, a previously captured French ship,
gained glory in the Battle of Trafalgar, 1805.
In 1838, whilst the ship was being towed down
the Thames to be scrapped, Turner painted his
famous picture. This inspired Sir Henry
Newbolt to write his poem. The tune is
in Music Hall style, an entertainment
popular in his day. The words
have been abridged.

La Belle Dame Sans Merci

Words: John Keats; music: Michael Raven

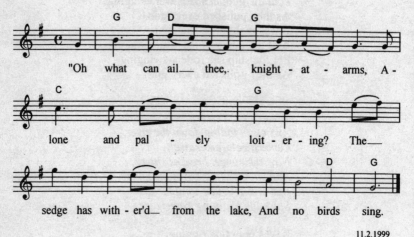

"Oh what can ail— thee, knight-at-arms, A-lone and pal-ely loit-er-ing? The— sedge has with-er'd— from the lake, And no birds sing.

11.2.1999

"O what can ail thee, knight-at-arms,
Alone and palely loitering?
The sedge has wither'd from the lake,
And no birds sing.

"O what can ail thee, knight-at-arms,
So haggard and so woe-begone?
The squirrel's granary is full,
And the harvest's done.

"I see the lily on thy brow
With anguish moist and fever-dew
And on thy cheeks a fading rose
Fast withereth too."

"I met a lady in the meads,
Full beautiful - a faery's child,
Her hair was long, her foot was light,
And her eyes were wild.

"I made a garland for her head,
And bracelets too, and fragrant zone;
She looked at me as she did love,
And made sweet moan.

"I set her on my pacing steed
And nothing else saw all day long,
For sidelong would she bend, and sing
A faery's song.

"She found me roots of relish sweet,
And honey wild and manna-dew,
And sure in language she said
'I love thee true.'

"She took me to her elfin grot,
And there she wept and sigh'd full sore,
And there I shut her wild, wild eyes
With kisses four.

"And there she lulled me asleep,
And there I dream'd - Ah! Woe betide!
The latest dream I ever dream'd
On the cold hill's side.

"I saw pale kings and princes too,
Pale warriors, death-pale were they all:
They cried - 'La belle Dame sans Merci
Hath thee in thrall!'

"I saw their starved lips in the gloam
With horrid warning gaped wide,
And I awoke and found me here
On the cold hill's side.

"And this is why I sojourn here,
Alone and palely loitering,
Though the sedge is wither'd from the lake,
And no birds sing."

Oh Where are you Going

Words: W. H. Auden; music: Michael Raven

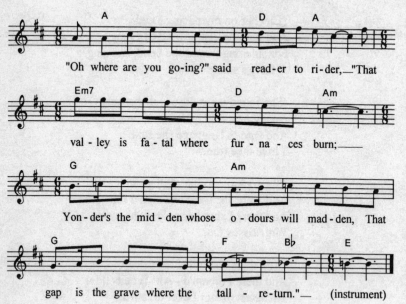

"Oh where are you go-ing?" said read-er to ri-der,—"That val-ley is fa-tal where fur-na-ces burn;— Yon-der's the mid-den whose o-dours will mad-den, That gap is the grave where the tall - re-turn."— (instrument)

"Oh where are you going?" said reader to rider,
"That valley is fatal where furnaces burn;
Yonder's the midden whose odours will madden,
That gap is the grave where the tall return."

"Oh do you imagine," said fearer to farer,
"That dusk will delay on your path to the pass,
Your diligent looking discover the lacking
Your footsteps will feel from granite to grass?"

"Oh what was that bird?" said horror to hearer,
"Did you see that shape in the twisted tree?
Behind you swiftly the figure comes softly,
The spot on your skin is a shocking disease."

"Out of this house" - said rider to reader,
"Yours never will," said farer to fearer,
"They're looking for you" - said hearer to horror,
As he left them there, as he left them there.

Earl Haldan's Daughter

Words: Charles Kingsley; music: Michael Raven

It was Earl. Hal-dan's daugh-ter, she looked a-cross the sea; She

looked a-cross the wa-ter; and long and loud laughed she: "The

locks of six prin-ces-ses must be my mar-riage fee, So

hey bon-ny boat, and ho bo-ny boat! who comes a-woo-ing me?"

15.10.1998

It was Earl Haldan's daughter, she looked across the sea;
She looked across the water; and long and loud laughed she:
"The locks of six princesses must be my marriage fee,
So hey bonny boat, and ho bonny boat! who comes a-wooing me?"

It was Earl Haldan's daughter, she walked along the sand;
When she was aware of a knight so fair, come sailing to the land.
His sails were all of velvet, his mast of beaten gold,
And "Hey bonny boat, and ho bonny boat! who saileth here so bold?"

"The locks of five princesses I won beyond the sea;
I clipt their golden tresses to fringe a cloak for thee.
One handful yet is wanting, but one of all the tale;
So hey bonny boat, and ho bonny boat! furl up thy velvet sail!"

He leapt into the water, that rover young and bold;
He gript Earl Haldan's daughter, he clipt her locks of gold:
"Go weep, go weep, proud maiden, the take is full today,
Now hey bonny boat, and ho bonny boat! sail Westward Ho! Away!"

Masque of Anarchy

Words: Percy Bysshe Shelley; music: Michael Raven

As I lay a-sleep in It-al-y

There came a voice from ov-er the sea, And with great power it

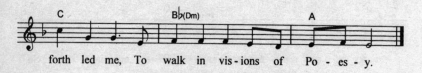

forth led me, To walk in vis-ions of Po-es-y.

As I lay asleep in Italy
There came a voice from over the sea,
And with great power it forth led me,
To walk in visions of Poesy.

I met Murder on the way -
He had a mask like Castlereagh -
Very smooth he looked, yet grim;
Seven bloodhounds followed him:

All were fat, and well they might
Be in admirable plight,
For one by one, and two by two,
He tossed them human hearts to chew.

Next came Fraud, and he had on,
Like Eldon, an ermined gown;
His big tears, for he wept well,
Turned to millstones as they fell.

And the little children, who
Round his feet played to and fro,
Thinking every tear a gem,
Had their brains knocked out by them.

Clothed with the Bible, as with light
And the shadows of the night,
Like Sidmouth, next, hypocrisy
On a crocodile rode by.

And many more Destruction played
In this ghastly masquerade,
All disguised, even to the eyes,
Like Bishops, lawyers, peers, or spies.

Last came Anarchy: he rode
On a white horse, splashed with blood;
He was pale even to the lips,
Like Death in the Apocalypse.

And he wore a kingly crown;
And in his grasp a sceptre shone;
On his brow this mark I saw -
"I AM GOD, AND KING, AND LAW!"

Never Seek

Words: William Blake; music: Michael Raven

Nev - er seek to tell thy love, Love that nev-er
told__ can be;____ For the gen - tle wind__ does__
move Sil - ent - ly in - vis - ib - ly.____

13.3.1999

Soon as she was gone from me
A traveller came by
Silently, invisibly -
O, was no deny.

I told my love, I told my love,
I told her all my heart,
Trembling, cold, in ghastly fears -
Ah, she doth depart.

Brothels of Paris

Words: William Blake; music: Michael Raven

"Let the broth - els___ of Par - is be open - ed,___

With man - y an al - lur - ing dance,

To a - wake the___ plague in the cit - y,"___

Said the beaut-ti - ful Queen of France. The King a - woke

on his couch of gold As soon as he heard these

tid - ing told: A - rise and come with both fife and drum,

The fa - mine shall eat both crust and crumb.

"Let the brothels of Paris be opened,
With many an alluring dance,
To awake the plague in the city,"
Said the beautiful Queen of France.

The King awoke on his couch of gold
As soon as he heard these tidings told:
Arise and come with both fife and drum,
The famine shall eat both crust and crumb.

Fayette beheld the Queen to smile
And to wink her lovely eye;
And soon he saw the pestilence
All from street to street to fly.

Fayette beheld the King and Queen
Standing in tears and iron bound;
But mute Fayette wept tear for tear,
And guarded them around.

Fayette, Fayette, thou wert bought and sold
And sold is thy happy morrow;
Thou gavest the tears of pity away
In exchange for the tears of sorrow.

O who would smile on the wintry seas,
And pity the stormy roar?
Or who will exchange his new born child
For the dog at the wintry door.

The Moon is Dead

**Words: based on Hilaire Belloc's The Moon's Funeral;
music: Michael Raven**

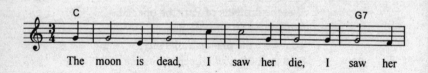

The moon is dead, I saw her die, I saw her

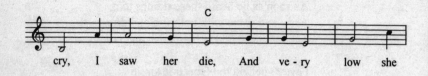

cry, I saw her die, And ve-ry low she

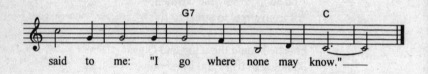

said to me: "I go where none may know."____

The moon is dead, I saw her die,
I saw her cry, I saw her die,
And very low she said to me:
"I go where none may know."

And will she never rise again,
Shine again, rise again?
Perhaps along the darkened shore,
Where pale ghosts are my love.

"I fade into a nameless land,
A lonely land, a nameless land.
I go where none may understand,
I fade away my love."

Magpies in Picardy

Words: T. P. Cameron-Wilson; music: Michael Raven

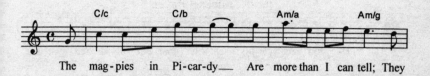

The mag-pies in Pi-car-dy— Are more than I can tell; They

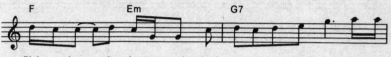

flick-er down— the dus-ty roads, And cast a ma-gic spell On the

men who march through Pi-car-dy, Through Pic-ar-dy to Hell.——

The magpies in Picardy
Are more than I can tell;
They flicker down the dusty roads,
And cast a magic spell
On the men who march through Picardy,
Through Picardy to Hell.

A magpie in Picardy
Told me secret things;
Of the magic of white feathers
And the sunlight that sings,
And dances in dark shadows,
He told me with his wings.

Cameron-Wilson was killed in action in
1918. There are more verses to this poem,
but none matches this high standard.
The small letters next to the chords in the
first line are bass notes. The tune was
made over this bass progression.

⁹⁴*from* The Ballad of Reading Gaol

Words: Oscar Wilde; music: Michael Raven

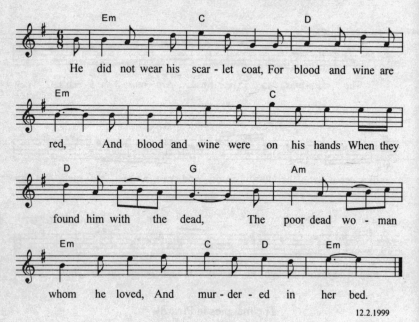

He did not wear his scar-let coat, For blood and wine are red, And blood and wine were on his hands When they found him with the dead, The poor dead wo-man whom he loved, And mur-der-ed in her bed.

12.2.1999

He did not wear his scarlet coat,
For blood and wine are red,
And blood and wine were on his hands
When they found him with the dead,
The poor dead woman whom he loved,
And murdered in her bed.

Dear Christ! The very prison walls
Suddenly seemed to reel,
And the sky above my head became
Like a casque of scorching steel;
And, though I was a soul in pain,
My pain I could not feel.

Yet each man kills the thing he loves,
By each let this be heard,
Some do it with a bitter look,
Some with a flattering word,
The coward does it with a kiss,
The brave man with a sword!

Some kill their love when they are young,
And some when they are old;
Some strangle with the hands of Lust,
Some with the hands of Gold:
The kindest use a knife, because
The dead so soon grow cold.

Some love too little, some too long,
Some sell, and others buy;
Some do the deed with many tears,
And some without a sigh:
For each man kills the thing he loves,
Yet each man does not die.

Sinner's Rue

Words: A. E. Housman; music: Michael Raven

I—— walked a - lone and—— th - ink - ing, And
faint the—— night - wind—— blew And stirred on—— mounds at
cro - ss - ways The flow'r of sin - ner's rue.

For where the roads part they bury
Him that his own hand slays,
And so the weed of sorrow
Springs at the four cross ways.

By night I picked it hueless,
When morning broke 'twas blue:
Blue at my breast I fastened
The flower of sinner's rue.

Dead clay that did me kindness,
I can do none to you,
But only wear for breastknot
The flower of sinner's rue.

To Carrey Clavel

Words: Thomas Hardy; music: Michael Raven
key G Mixolydian, drone on notes G and D throughout as in plainsong

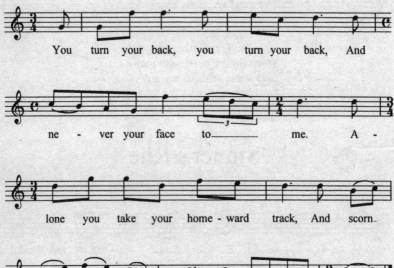

You turn your back, you turn your back, And

ne - ver your face to_____ me. A -

lone you take your home - ward track, And scorn

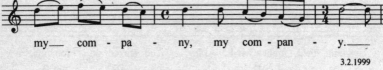

my__ com - pa - ny, my com - pan - y.__

3.2.1999

You turn your back, you turn your back,
And never your face to me.
Alone you take your homeward track,
And scorn my company.

What will you do, when Charley's seen,
Dew beating down this way,
You'll turn your back, as now you mean?
Nay, Carrey Clavel, nay.

You'll see none's looking, put your lip
Up like a tulip so
And he will coll you, bend and sip
Yes, Carrey, yes I know.

Shall We Go Dance?

Words: Nicholas Breton (?1545-1626); music: Michael Raven

Shall we go— dance the hay, the hay?

Nev - ver pipe could ev - er play Bet - ter shep - herd's

roun - de - lay, Bet - ter shep - herd's roun— de - lay.

1999

Shall we go dance the hay, the hay?
Never pipe could ever play
Better shepherd's roundelay.

Shall we go sing the song, the song?
Never Love did ever wrong.
Fair maids, hold hands all along.

Shall we go learn to woo, to woo?
Never thought came ever to,
Better deed could better do.

Shall we go learn to kiss, to kiss?
Never heart could ever miss
Comfort, where true meaning is.

Thus at base they run, they run,
When the sport was scarce begun.
But I waked, and all was done.

It fell upon an April day

Words: Francis Kilvert, from *Hill Flowers*; music: Michael Raven

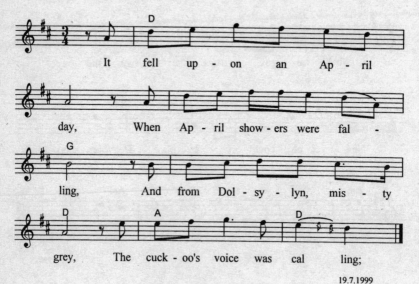

It fell up-on an Ap-ril day, When Ap-ril show-ers were fal-ling, And from Dol-sy-lyn, mis-ty grey, The cuck-oo's voice was cal-ling;

19.7.1999

It fell upon an April day,
When April showers were falling,
And from Dolsylyn, misty grey,
The cuckoo's voice was calling;

Beside the rippling winds of Wye,
So softly, swiftly flowing,
From fair Wyecliff to Llowes I
At eventide was going.

And when I reached the Otter's Pool,
The golden spires were sighing,
The hills were wrapped in rain, and cool
A white storm skudded flying;

Adown Cilceni's dingle side
The mountain rain was pouring,
Past Ty-ly-byngam deep and wide
The mountain brook was rouring.

The Darkling Thrush

Words: Thomas Hardy; music: Michael Raven

I leant_____ u - pon a_____ cop - pice
gate when fro - st was spec - tre - gr -
ey, And__ Win - ter's dregs made des - o -
late_____ the__ wea - ken - ing eye of day._____

25.1.1999

I leant upon a coppice gate when frost was spectre-grey,
And winter's dregs made desolate the weakening eye of day.
The tangled bine-stems scored the sky like strings of broken lyres,
And all mankind that haunted nigh had sought their household fires.

At once a voice arose among the bleak twigs overhead
In a full-hearted evensong of joy unlimited;
An aged thrush, frail, gaunt and small, in blast-beruffled plume,
Had chosen thus to fling his soul upon the growing gloom.

So little cause for carolings of such ecstatic sound
Was written on terrestrial things afar or near around,
That I could think there trembled through his happy good-night air
Some blessed hope, whereof he knew and I was unaware.

Count Arnaldos

Words: John Gibson Lockhart (1794-1854), from the Spanish
traditional ballad; music: Michael Raven

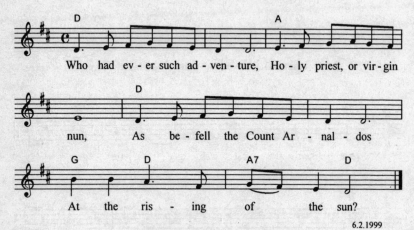

Who had ev - er such ad - ven - ture, Ho - ly priest, or vir - gin
nun, As be - fell the Count Ar - nal - dos
At the ris - ing of the sun?

6.2.1999

Who had ever such adventure,
Holy priest, or virgin nun,
As befell the Count Arnaldos
At the rising of the sun?

On his wrist the hawk was hooded,
Forth with horn and hound went he,
When he saw a stately galley
Sailing on the silent sea.

Sail of satin, mast of cedar,
Burnished decks of beaten gold -
Many a morn you'll hood your falcon
Ere you such a ship behold.

Sails of satin, masts of cedar,
Golden decks may come again,
But mortal ear no more shall listen
To yon grey-haired sailor's strain

Heart may beat, and eye may glisten,
Faith is strong and hope is free,
But mortal ear no more shall listen
To the song that rules the sea.

When the grey-haired sailor chaunted,
Every wind was hushed to sleep -
Like a virgin's bosom panted
All the wide reposing deep.

Bright in beauty rose the star-fish
From her green cave down below,
High above the eagle poised him -
Holy music charmed them so.

"Stately galley! glorious galley!
God hath poured His grace on thee!
Thou alone may'st scorn the perils
Of the dread devouring sea."

False Almeria's reefs and shallows,
Black Gibraltar's giant rocks,
Sound and sand-bank, gulf and whirl-pool,
All - my glorious galley mocks."

"For the sake of God, our Maker!"
Count Arnaldos' cry was strong.
"Old man, let me be partaker
In the secret of of thy song."

"Count Arnaldos! Count Arnaldos!
Hearts I read and thoughts I know -
Would'st thou learn the ocean's secret,
In our galley thou must go."

Nicholas Nye

Words: Walter de la Mare; music: Michael Raven

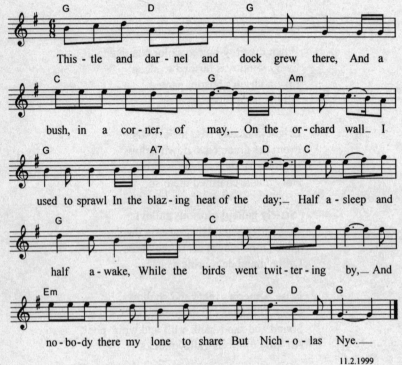

This - tle and dar - nel and dock grew there, And a
bush, in a cor - ner, of may,— On the or - chard wall— I
used to sprawl In the blaz - ing heat of the day;— Half a - sleep and
half a - wake, While the birds went twit - ter - ing by,— And
no - bo - dy there my lone to share But Nich - o - las Nye.—

11.2.1999

Thistle and darnel and dock grew there,
And a bush, in the corner, of may,
On the orchard wall I used to sprawl
In the blazing heat of the day;
Half asleep and half awake,
While the birds went twittering by,
And nobody there my lone to share
But Nicholas Nye.

Nicholas Nye was lean and grey,
Lame of a leg and old,
More than a score of donkey's years
He had seen since he was foaled;
He munched the thistles, purple and spiked,
Would sometimes stoop and sigh,
And turn to his head, as if he said,
"Poor Nicholas Nye!"

Alone with his shadow he'd drowse in the meadow,
Lazily swinging his tail,
At break of day he used to bray,
Not much too hearty and hale;
But a wonderful gumption was under his skin,
And a clear calm light in his eye,
And once in a while he'd smile -
Would Nicholas Nye.

Seem to be smiling at me, he would,
From his bush, in the corner, of may -
Bony and ownerless, widowed and worn,
Knobble-kneed, lonely and grey;
And over the grass would seem to pass
'Neath the deep dark blue of the sky,
Something much better than words between me
And Nicholas Nye.

But dusk would come in the apple boughs,
The green of the glow-worm shine,
The birds in nest would crouch to rest,
And home I'd trudge to mine;
And there, in the moonlight, dark with dew,
Asking not wherefore not why,
Would brood like a ghost, and as still as a post,
Old Nicholas Nye.

The Goose

Words: Alfred, Lord Tennyson; music: Michael Raven

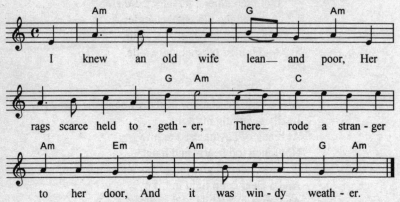

I knew an old wife lean and poor, Her
rags scarce held to-geth-er; There rode a stran-ger
to her door, And it was win-dy weath-er.

I knew an old wife lean and poor,
Her rags scarce held together;
There rode a stranger to her door,
And it was windy weather.

He held a goose upon his arm,
He uttered rhyme and reason,
"Here, take the goose, and keep you warm,
It is a stormy season."

She caught the white goose by the leg,
A goose - 'twas no great matter,
The goose let fall a golden egg
With crackle and with clatter.

She dropped the goose and caught the pelf,
And ran to tell her neighbours;
And blessed herself, and cursed herself,
And rested from her labours.

And feeling high, and living soft,
Grew plump and able-bodied;
Until the grave churchwarden doffed,
The parson smirked and nodded.

So sitting, served by man and maid,
She felt her heart grow prouder;
But ah! The more the white goose laid
It clacked and cackled louder.

It cluttered here, it chuckled there;
It stirred the old wife's mettle;
She shifted in her elbow chair,
And hurled the pan and kettle.

"A quinsy choke thy cursed note!"
Then waxed her anger stronger.
"Go, take the goose, and wring her throat,
I will not bear it longer."

Then yelped the cur, and yawled the cat;
Ran Gaffer, stumbled Gammer,
The goose flew this way and flew that,
And filled the house with clamour.

As head and heels upon the floor
They floundered all together,
There rode a stranger to the door,
And it was windy weather.

He took the goose upon his arm,
He uttered words of scorning;
"So keep you cold, or keep you warm,
It is a stormy morning."

The wild wind rang from park and plain,
And round the attics rumbled,
Till all the tables danced again,
And half the chimneys tumbled.

The glass blew in, the fire blew out,
The blast was hard and harder.
Her cap blew off, her gown blew up,
And a whirlwind cleared the larder.

And while on all sides breaking loose
Her household fled the danger,
Quoth she, "The Devil take the goose,
And God forget the stranger!"

Daffodils

Words: William Wordsworth; music: Michael Raven

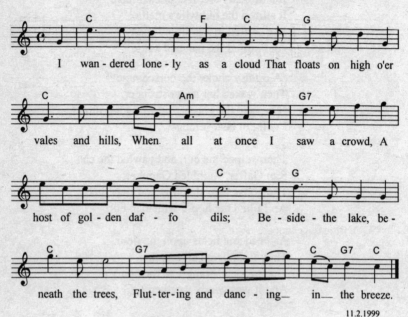

I wan-dered lone-ly as a cloud That floats on high o'er vales and hills, When all at once I saw a crowd, A host of gol-den daf - fo dils; Be - side - the lake, be-neath the trees, Flut-ter-ing and danc - ing— in— the breeze.

11.2.1999

Continuous as the stars that shine
And twinkle on the Milky Way,
They stretched in never-ending line
Along the margin of a bay:
Ten thousand saw I at a glance,
Tossing their heads in sprightly dance.

The waves beside them danced, but they
Outdid the sparkling waves in glee:
A poet could not but be gay,
In such a jocund company:
I gazed - and gazed - but little thought
What wealth the show to me had brought:

For oft, when on my couch I lie
In vacant or in pensive mood,
They flash upon that inward eye
Which is the bliss of solitude;
And then my heart with pleasure fills
And dances with the daffodils.

The Little Dog's Day

Words: Robert Brooke; music: Michael Raven

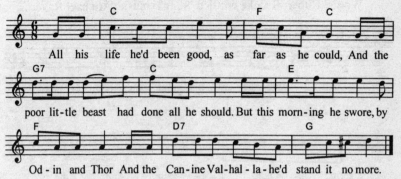

All his life he'd been good, as far as he could, And the poor lit-tle beast had done all he should. But this morn-ing he swore, by Od-in and Thor And the Can-ine Val-hal-la-he'd stand it no more.

3.2.1999

Spoken: All in the town were still asleep, when the sun came
up with a shout and a leap. In the lonely streets unseen by man,
a little dog danced. And the day began.

All his life he'd been good, as far as he could,
And the poor little beast had done all that he should.
But this morning he swore, by Odin and Thor
And the Canine Valhalla - he'd stand it no more!

So his prayer he got granted - to do just what he wanted,
Prevented by none, for the space of one day.
'Jam incipiebo, sedere facebo,'
In dog-Latin he quoth, 'Euge! Sophos! Hurray!'

He fought with the he-dogs, and winked at the she-dogs,
A thing that had never been heard of before.
'For the stigma of gluttony, I care not a button!' he
Cried, and ate all he could swallow - and more.

He took sinewy lumps from the shins of old frumps,
And mangled the errand-boys - when he could get 'em.
He shammed furious rabies, and bit all the babies,
And followed the cats up the trees, and then ate 'em!

They thought 'twas the devil was holding a revel,
And sent for the parson to drive him away;
For the town never knew such a hullabaloo
As that little dog raised - till the end of that day.

Spoken: When the blood-red sun had gone burning down,
and the lights were lit in the little town, outside, in the gloom
of the twilight grey, the little dog died when he'd had his day.

All Suddenly

Words: Rupert Brooke entitled 'Song'; music: Michael Raven

All sud-den-ly the wind comes soft, And spring is here a-gain; And the haw-thorn quick-ens with buds of green, And my heart with buds of pain.

3.2.1999

All suddenly the wind comes soft,
And Spring is here again;
And the hawthorn quickens with buds of green,
And my heart with buds of pain.

My heart all Winter lay so numb,
The earth so dead and frore,
That I never thought the Spring would come,
Or my heart wake any more.

But Winter's broken and earth has woken,
And the small birds cry again;
And the hawthorn hedge puts forth its buds,
And my heart puts forth its pain.

As I Walked Out One Evening

Words: Wystan Hugh Auden; music: Michael Raven

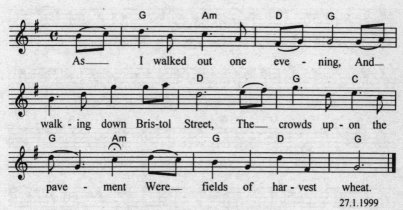

27.1.1999

As I walked out one evening,
And walking down Bristol Street,
The crowds upon the pavement
Were fields of harvest wheat.

And down by the brimming river
I heard a lover sing
Under an arch of the railway:
"Oh Love has no ending."

But all the clocks in the city
Began to whirr and chime:
'O let not Time deceive you,
You cannot conquer Time.

'In the burrows of the nightmare
Where Justice naked is,
Time watches from the shadow
And coughs when you would kiss.

'O look, look in the mirror,
O look in your distress;
Life remains a blessing
Although you cannot bless.'

It was late, late in the evening.
The lovers they were gone;
The clocks had ceased their chiming,
And the deep river ran on.

Roundabouts and Swings

Words: Patrick Chalmers; music: Michael Raven

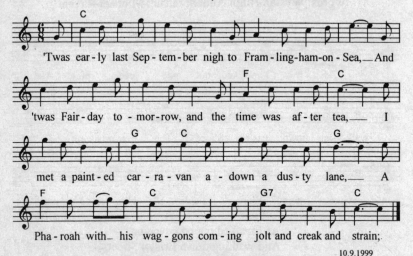

'Twas ear-ly last Sep-tem-ber nigh to Fram-ling-ham-on-Sea,— And 'twas Fair-day to-mor-row, and the time was af-ter tea,— I met a paint-ed car-ra-van a-down a dus-ty lane,— A Pha-roah with— his wag-gons com-ing jolt and creak and strain;

10.9.1999

'Twas early last September nigh to Framlingham-on-Sea,
And 'twas Fair-day tomorrow, and the time was after tea,
I met a painted caravan adown a dusty lane,
A Pharaoh with his waggons coming jolt and creak and strain;
A cheery cove and sunburnt, bold of eye and wrinkled up;
And beside him on the splashboard sat a brindled terrier pup,
And a lurcher wise as Solomon and lean as fiddle-strings
Was jogging in the dust along his roundabouts and swings.

"Good-day," said he; "Good-day," said I; "and how d'you find things go,
And what's the chance of millions when you runs a travelling show?"
"I find," said he, "things very much as how I've always found,
For mostly they goes up and down or else goes round and round."
Said he, "The job's the very spit of what it always were,
It's bread and bacon mostly when the dog don't catch a hare;
But looking at it broad, and while it ain't no merchant king's,
What's lost upon the roundabouts we pulls up on the swings!"

"Good luck," said he; "Good luck," said I; "you've put it past a doubt;
And keep that lurcher on the road, the gamekeeper is out;"
He thumped upon the footboard and he lumbered on again
To meet a gold-dust sunset down the owl-light in the lane;
And the moon she climbed the hazels, while a night-jar seemed to spin
That Pharaoh's wisdom o'er again, 'is sooth of lose-and-win;
For "up and down and round" said he, "goes all appointed things,
And losses on the roundabouts means profits on the swings!"

Dirge in Cymbeline

Words: William Collins (1721-1759); music: Michael Raven

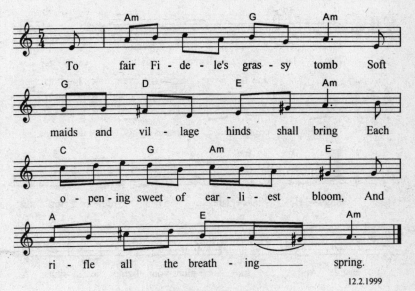

12.2.1999

To Fair Fidele's grassy tomb
Soft maids and village hinds shall bring
Each opening sweet of earliest bloom,
And rifle all the breathing spring.

No wailing ghost shall dare appear
To vex with shrieks this quiet grove;
But shepherd lads assemble here,
And melting virgins own their love.

No withered witch shall here be seen,
No goblins lead their nightly crew:
The female fays shall haunt the green,
And dress thy grave with pearly dew!

The red-breast oft at evening hours
Shall kindly lend his little aid:
With hoary moss and gathered flowers,
To deck the ground where thou art laid.

When howling winds and beating rain
In tempests shake the sylvan cell,
Or midst the chase on every plain,
The tender thought on thee shall dwell.

Larkrise

Words: Sir William Davenant (1606-1668); music: Michael Raven

The lark now leaves his watery nest,
And climbing shakes his dewy wings:
He takes this window for the east,
And to implore your light he sings:
Awake, awake, the morn will never rise,
'Till she can dress her beauty at your eyes!

The merchant bows unto the seaman's star,
The ploughman from his season takes;
But still the lover wonders what they are
Who look for day before his mistress wakes:
Awake, awake, break through your veils of lawn!
Then draw your curtains and begin the dawn.

Hell in Herefordshire

Words: *Punch,* 1921; music: Michael Raven

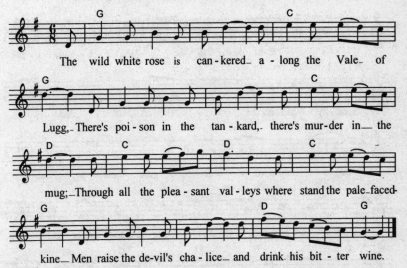

The wild white rose is can-kered_ a-long the Vale_ of Lugg,_ There's poi-son in the tan-kard,_ there's mur-der in_ the mug;_ Through all the plea-sant val-leys where stand the pale_faced_ kine_ Men raise the de-vil's cha-lice_ and drink his bit-ter wine.

16.1.1999

The wild white rose is cankered along the Vale of Lugg,
There's poison in the tankard, there's murder in the mug;
Through all the pleasant valleys where stand the palefaced kine
Men raise the devil's chalice and drink his bitter wine.

Unspeakable carouses that shame the summer sky
Take place in little houses that look towards the Wye;
And near the Radnor border and those dark hills of Wales
Beelzebub is warder and sorcery prevails.

For spite of church or chapel ungodly folk there be
Who pluck the cider apple from the cider apple tree,
And squeeze it in their presses until the juice runs out,
At various addresses that no-one knows about.

And, maddened by the orgies of that unholy brew
They slit each other's gorges from one a.m. till two,
Till Ledbury is a shambles and in the dirt and mud
Where Le'm'ster sits and gambles the dice are stained with blood.

But still, if strength suffices before my day is done,
I'll go and share the vices of Clungunford and Clun,
But watch the red sun sinking across the March again
And join the secret drinking of outlaws at Presteign.

Sea Fever

Words: John Masefield; music: Michael Raven

18.2.1999

I must down to the seas again, to the lonely sea and the sky,
And all I ask is a tall ship and a star to guide her by,
And the wheel's kick and the wind's song and the white sail's
    shaking,
And a grey mist on the sea's face, and a grey dawn breaking.

I must down to the seas again, for the call of the running tide
Is a wild call and a clear call that may not be denied;
And all I ask is a windy day with the white clouds flying,
And the flung spray and the blown spume, and the sea-gulls
    crying.

I must down to the seas again, to the vagrant gipsy life,
To the gull's way and the whale's way where the wind's like a
    whetted knife;
And all I ask is a merry yarn from a laughing fellow rover,
And quiet sleep and a sweet dream when the long trick's over.

Three Fishers

Words: Charles Kingsley; music: Michael Raven

Three fish-ers went sail-ing a-way to the West, A-way to the West as the sun went down: Each thought on the wo-man who loved him the best, And the chil-dren stood watch-ing them out of the town; For men must work, and wo-men must weep, And there's lit-tle to earn, and ma-ny to keep, Though the har-bour bar be moan-ing.

14.10.1998

Three wives sat up in the lighthouse tower,
And they trimmed the lamps as the sun went down;
They looked at the squall, and they looked at the shower,
And the night-rack came rolling up ragged and brown.
But men must work, and women must weep,
Though storms be sudden, and waters deep,
And the harbour bar be moaning.

Three corpses lay out on the shining sands
In the morning gleam as the tide went down,
And the women are weeping and wringing their hands
For those who will never come home to the town;
For men must work, and women must weep,
And the sooner it's over, the sooner to sleep,
And goodbye to the bar and its moaning.

The Garden

Words: Ron Baxter of Fleetwood; music: restructured traditional
phrases by Michael Raven

Born and died to-geth-er, we who ne-ver played
In the warmth of sum-mer, for we had no child-hood days; No
lov-ing arms ere held us, no moth-er's smil-ing face, On-ly the
cold and si-lent earth our bo-dies to em-brace.

26.2.1999

Born and died together, we who never played
In the warmth of summer, for we had no childhood days;
No loving arms ere held us, no mother's smiling face,
Only the cold and silent earth our bodies to embrace.

For we were never wanted, but for that we are not to blame,
And just like Herod's Innocents by cruel hands we're slain,
Buried in the garden, by mothers never seen,
There we were forgotten, as though we'd never been.

Yes, for the price of silver, and for the price of scorn,
Denied we were our mother's milk; condemned ere we were born.
Should we hate these murderers, these young girls full of fear?
Or those men who them betrayed, or those who brought them here?

Now who is there to grieve for us or to shed a tear?
For those who play upon our graves do not know we're here.
Yes, we're buried in the garden beneath the flowers gay,
Yes, we're buried in the garden where now other children play.

*An early 19th century graveyard containing the bodies of some 20 infants
was discovered by a farmer digging in his garden at Natelby, Lancashire.*

from Locksley Hall

Words: Alfred Tennyson; music: Michael Raven

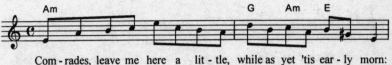

Com-rades, leave me here a lit-tle, while as yet 'tis ear-ly morn:

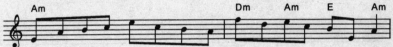

Leave me here, and when you want me, sound up-on your bug-le-horn.

'Tis the place, and all a-round it, as of old, the cur-lews call,

Drea-ry gleams a-bout the moor-land fly-ing o-ver Lock-sley Hall.

Comrades, leave me here a little, while as yet 'tis early morn:
Leave me here, and when you want me, sound upon your bugle-horn.
'Tis the place, and all around it, as of old, the curlews call,
Dreary gleams about the moorland flying over Locksley Hall.

Many an evening by the waters did we watch the stately ships,
And our spirits rushed together at the touching of our lips.
O my cousin, shallow-hearted! O my Amy, mine no more!
O the dreary, dreary moorland! O the the barren, barren shore!

I remember one that perished; sweetly did speak and move:
Such a one do I remember, whom to look at was to love.
Can I think of her as dead, and love her for the love she bore?
No - she never loved me truly: love is love for evermore.

Droops the heavy-blossomed bower, hangs the heavy-fruited tree -
Summer isles of Eden lying in dark-purple spheres of sea.
Howsoever these things be, a long farewell to Locksley Hall!
Now for me the woods may wither, now for me the roof-tree fall.

Old Dublin Fireman

Words: Ron Baxter; music: traditional, fitted and adapted
by Michael Raven

Stitched up in can - vas,_ a___ weight at his feet,

Wrapped in our en - sign,_ con - signed to the deep. The

en - gine was si - lent,_ the_ wind played an aire, As it

blew through the rig - ging,_ as we left you there. You

Old Dub - lin Fire - man_ who'd told us the tales, Of the

con - voys, the U - boats, the Bear Is - land gales, With

tan - kers a - blaz - ing,_ turn - ing night in - to day, You

Old Dub - lin Fire - man,_ you sure earned your_ pay.

Stitched up in canvas, a weight at his feet,
Wrapped in our ensign, consigned to the deep.
The engine was silent, the wind played an air,
As it blew through the rigging, as we left you there.

Chorus:
You old Dublin Fireman, who'd told us the tales,
Of the convoys, the U-boats, the Bear Island gales,
With tankers a-blazing, turning night into day,
You old Dublin Fireman, you sure earned your pay.

But why had you sailed 'neath Britain's red flag?
Eire was neutral and peace could be had;
You'd no love of the British as your Fenian songs tell,
Yet you sailed on those convoys to Murmansk and Hell.

The questions we'd ask, you'd reply with a smile:
"You can't sail a tanker 'cross Erin's green isle."
You'd then change the subject, starting shooting a line,
And leave us all guessing the reason you signed.

You sailed forty years, now your voyage it is through,
And marked on the chart is the spot we left you;
Stitched up in canvas, your beads in your hand,
Wrapped up in our flag, far from Erin's green land.

Going Home to Donegal

Words: P. McGill; music: Anglo-Irish traditional,
adapted and arranged by Michael Raven

I'm— go-ing back to— Glen-ties when the har-vest fields are—

brown, And the Aut-umn sun-set— lin-gers on my—

lit - tle— Ir - ish town, When the gos-sa-mer is—

shin-ing where the— moor-land— blos-soms— blow I'll—

take the road a - cross the hills I— tramped so— long a-

go - 'Tis— far I am be - yond the seas, but—

yearn-ing voi-ces call, "Will you not come back to—

Glen - ties, and your wave-washed Don-e - gal?"

I'm going back to Glenties when the harvest fields are brown,
And the Autumn sunset lingers on my little Irish town,
When the gossamer is shining where the moorland blossoms
   blow
I'll take the road across the hills I tramped so long ago -
'Tis far I am beyond the seas, but yearning voices call,
"Will you not come back to Glenties, and your wave-washed
   Donegal?"

I've seen the hopes of childhood stifled by the hand of time,
I've seen the smile of innocence become the frown of crime,
I've seen the wrong rise high and strong, I've seen the fair
   betrayed,
Until the faltering heart fell low, the brave became afraid -
But still the cry comes out to me, the homely voices call,
From the Glen among the highlands of my ancient Donegal.

Sure, I think I see them often, when the night is on the town,
The Braes of old Strasala, and the homes of Carrigdoun -
There's a light in Jimmy Lynch's house, a shadow on the
   blind,
I often watched the shadow, for 'twas Mary in behind,
And often in the darkness 'tis myself that sees it all,
For I cannot help but dreaming of the folk in Donegal.

So I'll hie me back to Glenties when the harvest comes again,
And the kine are in the pasture and the berries in the lane,
Then they'll give me such a welcome back that my heart will
   leap with joy,
When a father and a mother welcome back their wayward boy.
So I'm going back to Glenties when the autumn showers fall,
And the harvest home is cheery in my dear old Donegal.

Lucy

Words: selected from a poem by William Wordsworth; music:
traditional, Michael Raven. (Lucy died aged three.)

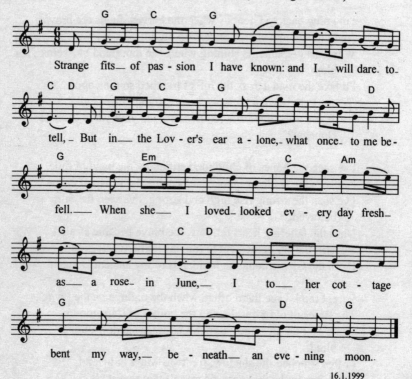

Strange fits— of pas - sion I have known: and I— will dare. to—
tell, — But in— the Lov - er's ear a - lone, — what once— to me befell.— When she— I loved— looked ev - ery day fresh—
as— a rose— in June, — I to— her cot - tage
bent my way,— be - neath— an eve - ning moon..

16.1.1999

Strange fits of passion have I known: and I will dare to tell,
But in the Lover's ear alone, what once to me befell.
When she I loved looked every day fresh as a rose in June,
I to her cottage bent my way, beneath an evening moon.

She dwelt among the untrodden ways beside the springs of Dove,
A maid whom there were none to praise and very few to love:
She lived unknown, and few could know when Lucy ceased to be;
But she is in her grave, and oh, the difference to me!

I travelled among unknown men, in lands beyond the sea;
Nor England! did I know till then what love I bore to thee.
They mornings showed, thy nights concealed, the bowers where
        Lucy played;
And thine too is the last green field that Lucy's eyes surveyed.

When I was one and twenty

Words: A. E. Housman; music: traditional, fitted by Michael Raven

When— I was one— and twent - y— I

heard a wise man say,——— "Give crowns and pounds and

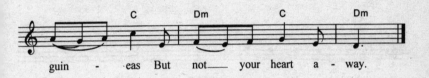

guin - eas But not— your heart a - way.

When I was one-and-twenty
I heard a wise man say,
"Give crowns and pounds and guineas
But not your heart away;

2Give pearls away and rubies
But keep your fancy free."
But I was one-and-twenty,
No use to talk to me.

When I was one-and-twenty
I heard him say again,
"The heart out of the bosom
Was never given in vain;

"'Tis paid with sighs a plenty
And sold for endless rue."
And I am two-and-twenty,
And oh, 'tis true, 'tis true.

Here dead lie we because we did not choose

Words: A. E. Housman; music: Michael Raven

Here dead we lie be - cause we did not choose To live and shame the land from which we sprung. Life, to be sure, is noth - ing much to lose; But young men think it is, and we were young.

Here dead lie we because we did not choose
To live and shame the land from which we sprung.
Life, to be sure, is nothing much to lose;
But young men think it is, and we were young.

First of May

Words: A. E. Housman; music: Michael Raven

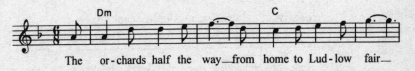

The or-chards half the way—from home to Lud-low fair—

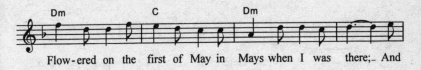

Flow-ered on the first of May in Mays when I was there;— And

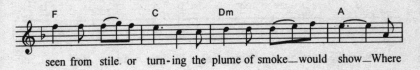

seen from stile. or turn-ing the plume of smoke—would show—Where

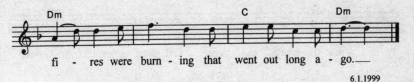

fi - res were burn - ing that went out long a - go.—

6.1.1999

The orchards half the way from home to Ludlow fair
Flowered on the first of May in Mays when I was there;
And seen from stile or turning the plume of smoke would show
Where fires were burning that went out long ago.

The plum broke forth in green, the pear stood high and snowed,
My friends and I between would take the Ludlow road;
Dressed to the nines and drinking and light in heart and limb,
And each chap thinking the fair was held for him.

Between the trees in flower new friends at fairtime tread
The way where Ludlow tower stands planted on the dead.
Our thoughts, a long while after, they think, our words they say;
Their's now the laughter, the fair, the first of May.

Ay, yonder lads are yet the fools that we were then;
For oh, the sons we get are still the sons of men.
The sumless tale of sorrow is all unrolled in vain:
May comes tomorrow and Ludlow fair again.

Hughley Steeple

Words: A. E. Housman; music: Michael Raven

The vane on Hugh-ley stee-ple veers bright, a far—known sign,_____ And there lie Hugh-ley peo-ple, and_____ there lie—friends of mine. Tall in their midst the tow-er di-vides the shade and sun, And the clock_____ strikes the hour_____ and_____ tells_____ the_____ time to none.

20.2.1999

The vane on Hughley steeple veers bright, a far known sign,
And there lie Hughley people, and there lie friends of mine.
Tall in their midst the tower divides the shade and sun,
And the clock strikes the hour and tells the time to none.

To the south the headstones cluster, the sunny mounds lie thick;
The dead are more in muster at Hughley than the quick.
North, for a soon-told number, chill graves the sexton delves,
And steeple-shadowed slumber the slayers of themselves.

To north, to south, lie parted, with Hughley tower above,
The kind, the single-hearted, the lads I used to love.
And, south or north, 'tis only a choice of friends one knows,
And I shall ne'er be lonely asleep with these or those.

The Lent Lily

Words: A. E. Housman; music: Michael Raven

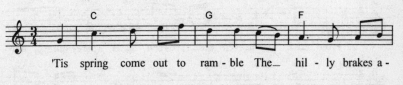

'Tis spring come out to ram - ble The— hil - ly brakes a -

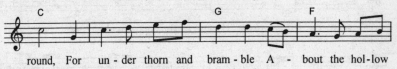

round, For un - der thorn and bram - ble A - bout the hol - low

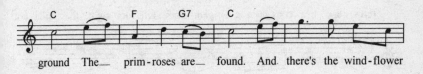

ground The— prim - roses are— found. And. there's the wind - flower

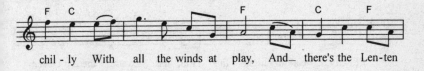

chil - ly With all the winds at play, And— there's the Len - ten

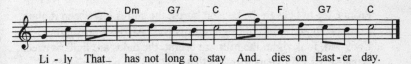

Li - ly That— has not long to stay And— dies on East - er day.

8.1.1999

'Tis spring come out to ramble
The hilly brakes around,
For under thorn and bramble
About the hollow ground
The primroses are found.

And there's the windflower
    chilly
With all the winds at play,
And there's the Lenten lily
That has not long to stay
And dies on Easter day.

And since till girls go maying
You find the primrose still,
And find the windflower
    playing
With every wind at will,
But not the daffodil.

Bring baskets now, and sally
Upon the spring's array,
And bear from hill and valley
The daffodil away
That dies on Easter day.

1887

Words: A. E. Housman; music: Michael Raven

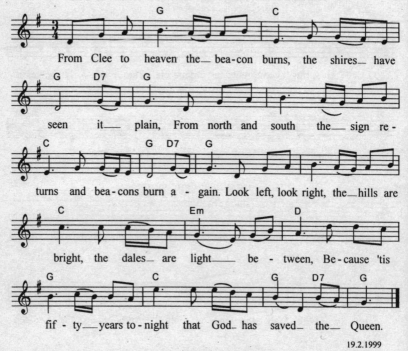

From Clee to heaven the— bea-con burns, the shires— have seen it— plain, From north and south the— sign re-turns and bea-cons burn a - gain. Look left, look right, the—hills are bright, the dales— are light—— be - tween, Be-cause 'tis fif - ty—years to-night that God— has saved— the— Queen.

19.2.1999

From Clee to heaven the beacon burns, the shires have seen it plain,
From north and south the sign returns and beacons burn again.
Look left, look right, the hills are bright, the dales are light between,
Because 'tis fifty years to-night that God has saved the Queen.

Now, when the flame they watch not towers about the soil they trod,
Lads, we'll remember friends of ours who shared the work of God.
To skies that knit their heartstrings right, to fields that bred them brave,
The saviours come not home tonight: themselves they could not save.

It dawns in Asia, tombstones show, and Shropshire names are read;
And the Nile spills his overflow beside the the Severn's dead.
We pledge in peace by farm and town the Queen they served in war,
And fire the beacons up and down the land they perished for.

"God save the Queen" we living sing, from height to height 'tis heard;
And with the rest your voices ring, Lads of the Fifty Third.
Oh, God will save her, fear you not: be you the men you've been,
Get you the sons your fathers got, and God will save the Queen.

Is My Team Ploughing?

Words: A. E. Housman; music: Michael Raven

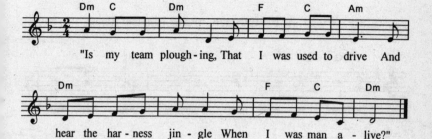

"Is my team plough-ing, That I was used to drive And
hear the har-ness jin-gle When I was man a-live?"

"Is my team ploughing,
That I was used to drive
And hear the harness jingle
When I was man alive?"

Ay, the horses trample,
The harness jingles now:
No change though you lie under
The land you used to plough.

"Is my girl happy,
That I thought hard to leave,
And has she tired of weeping
As she lies down at eve?"

Ay, she lies down lightly,
She lies not down to weep:
Your girl is well contented.
Be still, my lad, and sleep.

"Is my friend hearty,
Now I am thin and pine,
And has he found to sleep in
a better bed than mine?"

Yes, lad, I lie easy,
I lie as lads would choose;
I cheer a dead man's sweetheart,
Never ask me whose.

Epitaph on an Army of Mercenaries

Words: A. E. Housman; music: Michael Raven

These, in the day when heaven was falling,
The hour when earth's foundations fled,
Followed their mercenary calling
And took their wages and were dead.

Their shoulders held the sky suspended;
They stood, and earth's foundations stay;
What God abandoned, these defended,
And saved the sum of things for pay.

Lancer

Words: A. E. Housman; music: Michael Raven

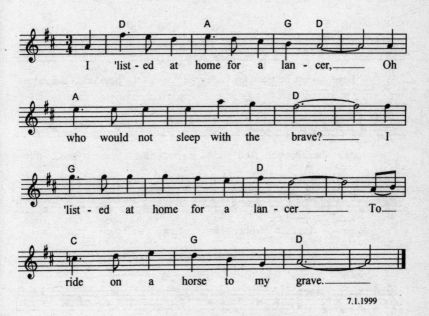

I 'list-ed at home for a lan-cer,_____ Oh who would not sleep with the brave?_____ I 'list-ed at home for a lan-cer_____ To_____ ride on a horse to my grave._____

7.1.1999

I 'listed at home for a lancer,
Oh who would not sleep with the brave?
I 'listed at home for a lancer
To ride on a horse to my grave.

And over the seas we were bidden
A country to take and to keep;
And far with the brave I have ridden,
And now with the brave I shall sleep.

For round me the men will be lying
That learned me the way to behave,
And showed me my business of dying:
Oh who would not sleep with the brave?

And I with the brave shall be sleeping
At ease on my mattress of loam,
And back from their taking and keeping
The squadron is riding at home.

Loveliest of Trees

Words: A. E. Housman; music: Michael Raven

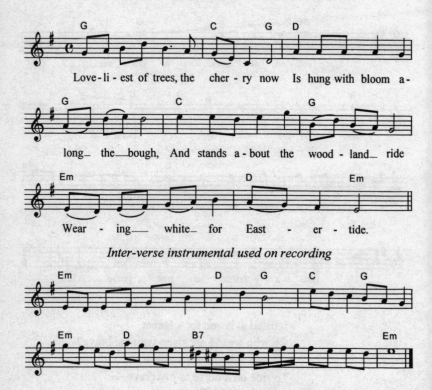

Love - li - est of trees, the cher - ry now Is hung with bloom a-

long— the—bough, And stands a - bout the wood - land— ride

Wear - ing— white— for East - er - tide.

Inter-verse instrumental used on recording

Loveliest of trees, the cherry now
Is hunggg with bloom along the bough,
And stands about the woodland ride
Wearing white for Eastertide.

Now, of my three score years and ten,
Twenty will not come again,
And take from seventy springs a score,
It only leaves me fifty more,

And since to look at things in bloom
Fifty springs are little room,
About the woodlands I will go
To see the cherry hung with snow.

Oh Fair Enough

Words: A. E. Housman; music: Michael Raven

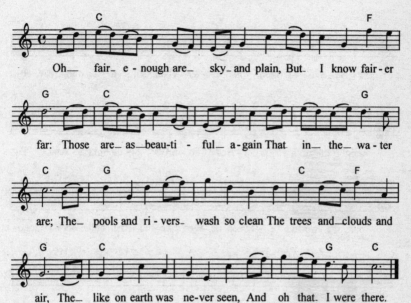

Oh— fair— e - nough are— sky— and plain, But— I know fair - er
far: Those are— as— beau-ti - ful— a - gain That in— the— wa - ter
are; The— pools and ri - vers— wash so clean The trees and—clouds and
air, The— like on earth was ne-ver seen, And oh that— I were there.

Oh fair enough are sky and plain,
But I know fairer far:
Those are as beautiful again
That in the water are;

The pools and rivers wash so clean
The trees and clouds and air,
The like on earth was never seen,
And oh that I were there.

These are the thoughts I often think
As I stand gazing down
In act upon the cressy brink
To strip and dive and drown;

But in the golden-sanded brooks
And azure meres I spy
A silly lad that longs and looks
And wishes he were I.

Because I Liked You Better

Words: A. E. Housman; music: Michael Raven

Be-cause I liked you bet-ter Than suits a man_ to say, It
irked you, and I prom-ised To throw the thought a-way. To
put the world_ be-tween us We part-ed, stiff and dry; "Goodbye," said you, "for-get me." "I will, no fear," said I.

Because I liked you better
Than suits a man to say,
It irked you, and I promised
To throw the thought away.

To put the world between us
We parted, stiff and dry;
"Good-bye," said you, "forget me."
"I will, no fear," said I.

If here, where clover whitens
The dead man's knoll, you pass,
And no tall flower to meet you
Starts in the trefoiled grass.

Halt by the headstone naming
The heart no longer stirred,
And say the lad that loved you
Was one that kept his word.

The Carpenter's Son

Words: A. E. Housman; music: Michael Raven

Here the hang-man stops his cart: Now the best of friends must part. Fare you well, for ill fare I: Live, lads, and I will die.

16.6.1999

Here the hangman stops his cart:
Now the best of friends must part.
Fare you well, for ill fare I:
Live, lads, and I will die.

Oh, at home had I but stayed
'Prentice to my father's trade,
Had I stuck to plane and adze,
I had not been lost, my lads.

Then I might have built perhaps
Gallows-trees for other chaps,
Never dangled on my own,
Had I but left ill alone.

Now, you see, they hang men high,
And the people passing by
Stop to shake their fists and curse;
So 'tis come from ill to worse.

Here hang I, and right and left
Two poor fellows hang for theft:
All the same's the luck we prove,
Though the midmost hangs for love.

Comrades all, that stand and gaze,
Walk henceforth in other ways;
See my neck and save your own:
Comrades all, leave ill alone.

Make some day a decent end,
Shrewder fellows than your friend.
Fare you well, for ill fare I:
Live, lads, and I will die.

Illic Jacet

Words: A. E. Housman; music: Michael Raven

Oh hard is the bed they have made— him, And com mon the blan-ket and cheap; But there he will lie as they laid— him: Where else could you trust him to sleep?— To sleep where the bu - gle is cry - ing And— cra - vens have heard and are brave, When mo - thers and sweet-hearts are sigh— ing And lads are in love with the grave.—

Oh hard is the bed they have made him,
And common the blanket and cheap;
But there he will lie as they laid him:
Where else could you trust him to sleep?
To sleep where the bugle is crying
And cravens have heard and are brave,
When mothers and sweethearts are sighing
And lads are in love with the grave.

Oh dark is the chamber and lonely,
And lights and companions depart:
But lief will he lose them and only
Behold the desire of his heart.
And low is the roof, but it covers
A sleeper content to repose;
And far from his friends and his lovers
He lies with the sweetheart he chose.

The West

Words: A. E. Housman; music: Michael Raven

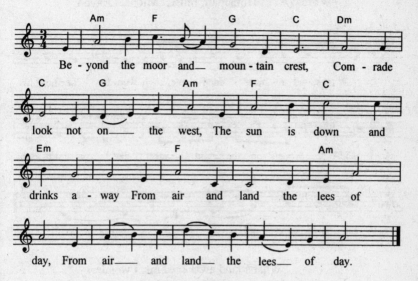

Be - yond the moor and— moun - tain crest, Com - rade
look not on— the west, The sun is down and
drinks a - way From air and land the lees of
day, From air— and land— the lees— of day.

The long cloud and the single pine
Sentinel the ending line,
And out beyond it, clear and wan,
Reach the gulfs of evening on.

Comrade, look not on the west:
'Twill have the heart out of your breast;
'Twill take your thoughts and sink them far,
Leagues beyond the sunset bar.

Oh lad, I fear that yon's the the sea
Where they fished for you and me,
And there, from whence we both were ta'en,
You and I shall drown again.

Wide is the world, to rest or roam,
And early is for turning home:
Plant your heel on earth and stand,
And let's forget your native land.

When you and I are spilt on air
Long we shall be strangers there;
Friends of flesh and bone are best:
Comrade, look not on the west.

The Deserter

Words: A. E. Housman; music: Michael Raven

What sound a - wak - ened me,— I won-der For now 'tis dumb?— Wheels on the road— most like,— or thun - der; Lie down, 'twas not—— the drum.——

'What sound awakened me, I wonder
For now 'tis dumb.'
'Wheels on the road most like, or thunder
Lie down; 'twas not the drum.'

Toil at sea and two in haven
And trouble far:
Fly, crow, away, and follow, raven,
And all that croaks for war.

'Hark, I heard the bugle crying,
And where am I?
My friends are up and dressed and dying,
And I will dress and die.'

'Oh love is rare and trouble plenty
And carrion cheap,
And daylight dear at four-and-twenty;
Lie down again and sleep.'

'Reach me my belt and leave your prattle:
Your hour is gone;
But my day is the day of battle,
And that comes dawning on.

'They mow the field of man in season:
Farewell, my fair,
And call it truth or call it treason,
Farewell the vows that were.'

'Ay, false heart, forsake me lightly:
'Tis like the brave.
They find no bed to joy in rightly
Before they find the grave.

'Their love is for their own undoing,
And east is west
They scour about the world a-wooing
The bullet to their breast.

'Sail away the ocean over,
Oh sail away,
And lie there with your leaden lover
For ever and a day.'

The Welsh Marches

Words: A. E. Housman; music: Michael Raven

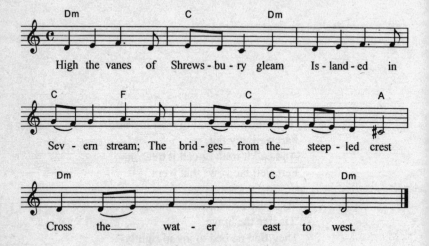

High the vanes of Shrewsbury gleam
Islanded in Severn stream;
The bridges from the steepled crest
Cross the water east to west.

The flag of morn in conqueror's state
Enters at the English gate:
The vanquished eve, as night prevails,
Bleeds upon the road to Wales.

Ages since the vanquished bled
Round my mother's marriage bed:
There the ravens feasted far
About the open house of war.

In my heart it has not died,
The war that sleeps on Severn side:
They cease not fighting, east and west,
On the Marches of my breast.

When shall I be dead and rid
Of the wrong my father did?
How long, how long, till spade and hearse
Put to sleep my mother's curse?

Thirteen Pence a Day

Words: A. E. Housman and traditional; music: Michael Raven

The Queen she sent to look for me, the ser-geant he did say, "Young man, a sol-dier will you be for thir-teen pence a day?" For thir-teen pence a day did I take off the things I wore, And I have marched to where I lie, and I shall march no more.

The Queen she sent to look for me, the sergeant he did say,
"Young man, a soldier will you be for thirteen pence a day?"
For thirteen pence a day did I take off the things I wore,
And I have marched to where I lie, and I shall march no more.

"Oh sign and be a soldier, lad, the Queen's work must be done;
Hark! Don't you hear the fife to play, the beating of the drum;"
And I shall have to bate my price, for in the grave they say,
Is neither knowledge nor device nor thirteen pence a day."

My mouth is dry, my shirt is wet, my blood runs all away,
So now I shall not die in debt for thirteen pence a day.
Tomorrow after new young men the sergeant he must see,
For things will all be over then between the Queen and me.

¹⁴² Farewell to barn and stack and tree

Words: A. E. Housman; music: traditional, fitted by Michael Raven

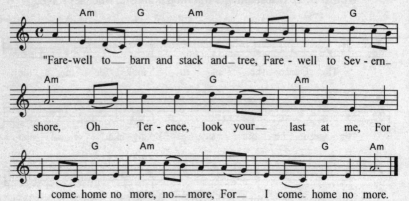

"Fare-well to— barn and stack and— tree, Fare - well to Sev - ern— shore, Oh— Ter - ence, look your— last at me, For I come home no more, no— more, For— I come home no more.

"Farewell to barn and and stack and tree,
Farewell to Severn shore,
Oh Terence, look your last at me,
For I come home no more, no more,
For I come home no more.

"The sun burns on the half-mown hill,
By now the blood is dried;
And Maurice amongst the hay lies still
And my knife is in his side, his side,
My knife is in his side.

"My mother thinks us long away;
'Tis time the fields were mown,
She had two sons at rising day,
Tonight she'll be alone, alone,
Tonight she'll be alone.

"And here's a bloody hand to shake,
And oh, man, here's goodbye;
We'll sweat no more on scythe and rake,
My bloody hands and I, and I,
My bloody hands and I.

"I wish you strength to bring you pride,
And a love to keep you clean,
And I wish you luck, come Lammastide,
At racing on the green, the green,
At racing on the green."

On Wenlock Edge

Words: A. E. Housman; music: traditional, fitted by Michael Raven

On Wen-lock Edge the wood's in trou - ble;____ His for - est fleece the Wre - kin heaves; The____ gale, it plies the sap - lings____ dou - ble,____ And____ thick on Sev - ern____ snow the____ leaves.

On Wenlock Edge the wood's in trouble;
His forest fleece the Wrekin heaves;
The gale, it plies the saplings double,
And thick on Severn snow the leaves.

'Twould blow like this through holt and hanger
When Uricon the city stood:
'Tis the old wind in the old anger,
But then it threshed another wood.

Then, 'twas before my time, the Roman
At yonder heaving hill would stare:
The blood that warms an English yoeman,
The thoughts that hurt him, they were there.

There, like the wind through woods in riot,
Through him the gale of life blew high;
The tree of man was never quiet:
Then 'twas the Roman, now 'tis I.

Along the Fields

Words: A. E. Housman; music: traditional, fitted by Michael Raven

A - long the fields as we came— by A

year a - go, my— love and I, The as - pen o - ver

stile and— stone Was talk - ing to it - self a - lone.

Along the fields as we came by
A year ago, my love and I,
The aspen over stile and stone
Was talking to itself alone.

Oh who are these that kiss and pass?
A country lover and his lass;
Two lovers looking to be wed;
And time shall put them both to bed.

But she shall lie with earth above,
And he beside another love.
And sure enough beneath the tree
There walks another love with me.

And overhead the aspen heaves
Its rainy-sounding silver leaves;
And I spell nothing in their stir,
But now perhaps they speak to her.

Land of Lost Content

Words: A. E. Housman; music: traditional, fitted, arranged
and adapted by Michael Raven

key G Mixolydian

With rue my heart is la-den For gol-den friends I had, For man-y a rose-lipt mai-den And man-y a light-foot lad. By brooks too broad. for leap-ing The light-foot boys are laid; The rose-lipt girls are sleep-ing In fields where ros-es fade.

With rue my heart is laden
For golden friends I had,
For many a rose-lipt maiden
And many a lightfoot lad.
By brooks too broad for leaping
The lightfoot boys are laid;
The rose-lipt girls are sleeping
In fields where roses fade.

Stanzas LIV
and XL from
*A Shropshire
Lad* are here
combined

Into my heart an air that kills
From yon far country blows;
What are those blue remembered hills,
What spires, what farms are those?
That is the land of lost content,
I see it shining plain,
The happy highways where I went
And cannot come again.

Wenlock Edge

Words: A. E. Housman; music: traditional, fitted by Michael Raven

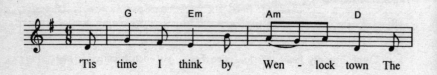

'Tis time I think by Wen - lock town The

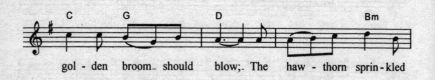

gol - den broom should blow; The haw - thorn sprin - kled

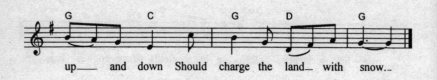

up and down Should charge the land with snow.

'Tis time I think by Wenlock town
The golden broom should blow;
The hawthorn sprinkled up and down
Should charge the land with snow.

Spring will not wait the loiterer's time
Who keeps so long away;
So others wear the broom and climb
The hedgerows heaped with may.

Oh tarnish late on Wenlock Edge,
Gold that I never see;
Lie long, high snowdrifts in the hedge
That will not shower on me.

Half Moon

Words: A. E. Housman; music: traditional, fitted by Michael Raven

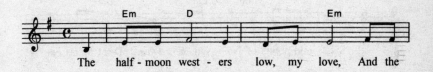

The half - moon west - ers low, my love, And the

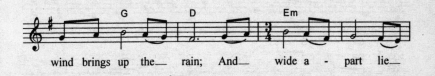

wind brings up the— rain; And— wide a - part lie—

we, my— love, And seas be - tween the— twain.

The half moon westers low, my love,
And the wind brings up the rain;
And wide apart lie we, my love,
And seas between the twain.

I know not if it rains, my love,
In the land where you do lie;
And oh, so sound you sleep, my love,
You know no more than I.

The sigh that heaves the grasses
Whence thou wilt never rise
Is of the air that passes
And knows not if it sighs.

The diamond tears adorning
Thy low mound on the lea,
Those are the tears of morning,
That weeps, but not for thee.

Midnights of November

Words: A. E. Housman; music: traditional, fitted by Michael Raven

In— mid-nights of No - vem-ber, when— Dead Man's Fair is
nigh, And— dan - ger in the val - ley, and—
an - ger in the sky. A - round the hud - dling
home - steads the leaf - less tim - ber roars, The
dead they call the dy - ing and— fin - ger at the doors.

In midnights of November, when Dead Man's Fair is nigh,
And danger in the valley, and anger in the sky.
Around the huddling homesteads the leafless timber roars,
The dead they call the dying and finger at the doors.

Oh, yonder faltering fingers are hands I used to hold;
Their false companion drowses and leaves them in the cold.
Oh, to the bed of ocean, to Africk and to Ind,
I will arise and follow along the rainy wind.

The night goes out and under with all its train forlorn;
Hues in the east assemble and cocks crow up the morn.
The living are the living and dead the dead will stay,
And I will sort with comrades that face the beam of day.

Come Pipe a Tune

Words: A. E. Housman; music: traditional Morris tune altered
and adapted by Michael Raven

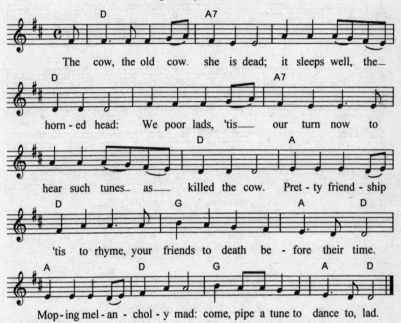

The cow, the old cow. she is dead; it sleeps well,. the— horn-ed head: We poor lads, 'tis— our turn now to hear such tunes— as— killed the cow. Pret-ty friend-ship 'tis to rhyme, your friends to death be-fore their time. Mop-ing mel-an-chol-y mad: come, pipe a tune to dance to, lad.

The cow, the old cow, she is dead; it sleeps well, the horned head:
We poor lads, 'tis our turn now to hear such tunes as killed the cow.
Pretty friendship 'tis to rhyme, your friends to death before their time.
Moping melancholy mad: come, pipe a tune to dance to, lad.

Why, if 'tis dancing you would be, there's brisker pipes than poetry.
Say, for what were hop-yards meant, or why was Burton built on Trent?
Oh many a peer of England brews livelier liquor than the Muse,
And malt does more than Milton can to justify God's ways to man.

Oh I have been to Ludlow fair and left my necktie God knows where,
And carried half-way home, or near, pints and quarts of Ludlow beer:
Then the world seemed none so bad, and I myself a sterling lad;
And down in lovely muck I've lain, happy till I woke again.

Therefore, since the world has still, much good, but much less good than ill,
And the sun and moon endure, luck's a chance, but trouble's sure.
I'd face it as a wise man would, and train for ill and not for good.
'Tis true, the stuff I bring for sale is not so brisk a brew as ale.

Ludlow Recruit

Words: A. E. Housman; music: traditional, fitted by Michael Raven

Oh, leave your home be - hind, lad,____ And reach your friends_ your hand,___ And go, and luck_ go with you___ While Lud - low tow - er shall stand.____

Oh, leave your home behind, lad,
And reach your friends, your hand,
And go, and luck go with you
While Ludlow tower shall stand.

Oh, come you home of Sunday
When Ludlow streets are still
And Ludlow bells are calling
To farm and lane and mill.

Or come you home of Monday
When Ludlow market hums
And Ludlow chimes are playing
"The conquering hero comes."

Come you home a hero,
Or come not home at all,
The lads you leave will mind you
Till Ludlow tower shall fall.

And you will list the bugle
That blows in lands of morn,
And make the foes of England
Be sorry you were born.

And you will trump of doomsday
On lands of morn may lie,
And make the hearts of comrades
Be heavy where you die.

Bredon Hill

Words: A. E. Housman;
music: traditional, arranged and adapted by Michael Raven

In summertime on Bredon the bells they sound so clear;
Round both the shires they ring them in steeples far and near.
Here of a Sunday morning my love and I would lie,
And see the coloured counties, and hear the larks so high.

The bells would ring to call her in valleys miles away:
"Come all to church, good people; good people, come and pray."
And I would turn and answer among the springing thyme
"O peal upon our wedding, and we will hear the chime."

But when the snows at Christmas on Bredon top were strown,
My love rose up so early and went to church alone.
They tolled the one bell only, groom there was none to see,
The mourners followed after, and so to church went she.

New Mistress

Words: A. E. Housman; music: traditional, adapted by Michael Raven

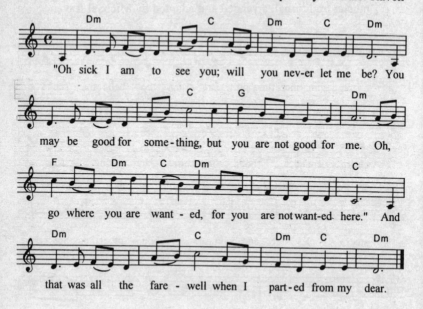

"Oh sick I am to see you; will you nev-er let me be? You
may be good for some-thing, but you are not good for me. Oh,
go where you are want-ed, for you are not want-ed here." And
that was all the fare-well when I part-ed from my dear.

Oh sick I am to see you; will you never let me be?
You may be good for something, but you are not good for me.
Oh, go where you are wanted, for you are not wanted here."
And that was all the farewell when I parted from my dear.

"I will go where I am wanted, to a lady born and bred
Who will dress me free for nothing in a uniform of red;
She will not be sick to see me if I only keep it clean:
I will go where I am wanted for a soldier of the Queen.

"I will go where I am wanted, for the sergeant does not mind;
He may be sick to see me but he treats me very kind:
He gives me beer and breakfast and a ribbon for my cap,
And I never knew a sweetheart spend her money on a chap.

"I will go where I am wanted, where there's room for one or
     two,
And the men are none too many for the work there is to do;
Where the standing line wears thinner and the dropping dead
     lie thick;
And the enemies of England they shall see me and be sick."

Shrewsbury Jail

Words: A. E. Housman music: traditional, fitted by Michael Raven

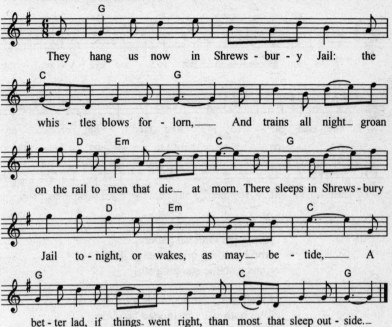

They hang us now in Shrews-bur-y Jail: the whis-tles blows for-lorn,—— And trains all night— groan on the rail to men that die— at morn. There sleeps in Shrews-bury Jail to-night, or wakes, as may— be-tide,—— A bet-ter lad, if things— went right, than most that sleep out-side.—

On moonlit heath and lonesome bank the sheep beside me graze;
And yon the gallows used to clank fast by the four cross ways.
A careless shepherd once would keep the flocks by moonlight there,
And high amongst the glimmering sheep the dead man stood on air.

They hang us now in Shrewsbury Jail: the whistles blow forlorn,
And trains all night groan on the rail to men that die at morn.
There sleeps in Shrewsbury Jail tonight, or wakes, as may betide,
A better lad, if things went right, than most that sleep outside.

And naked in the hangman's noose the morning clocks will ring
A neck god made for other use than strangling in a string.
And sharp the link of life will snap, and dead on air will stand
Heels that held as straight a chap as treads upon the land.

So here I'll watch the night and wait to see the morning shine,
When he will hear the stroke of eight and not the stroke of nine;
And wish my friend as sound a sleep as lads I did not know,
That shepherded the moonlit sheep a hundred years ago.

Loitering with a Vacant Eye

Words: A. E. Housman; music: part traditional, part Michael Raven

As loit-er-ing with a vac-ant eye A-long the
Gre-cian gal-le-ry, And brood-ing on my
hea-vy ill, I met a sta-tue stand-ing still.

As loitering with a vacant eye
Along the Grecian gallery,
And brooding on my heavy ill,
I met a statue standing still.

"Well met," I thought his look did say,
"We both were fashioned far away;
We neither knew when we were young,
These Londoners we live among."

And still he stood and eyed me hard,
An earnest and a grave regard:
"What, lad, drooping with your lot?
I too would be where I am not.

I too survey that endless line
Of men whose thoughts are not as mine.
The years, ere you stood up from the rest,
Hard on my neck the collar prest;

The years, when you lay down your ill,
Then I shall stand and bear it still.
Oh! Courage, lad, 'tis not for long:
Come stand, quit you like stone, be strong."

And so I thought his look would say;
And light on me my trouble lay,
And I stepped out in flesh and bone
So manful like the man of stone.

True Lover

Words: A. E. Housman; music: traditional, fitted by Michael Raven

The lad came to the door at night, when lov-ers crown their vows, And whist-led soft and out of sight in sha-dow of the boughs. I shall not vex you with my face hence-forth my love, for aye;— So take me in your arms a-space be - fore the east is grey.—

The lad came to the door at night, when lovers crown their vows,
And whistled soft and out of sight in shadow of the boughs.
I shall not vex you with my face henceforth my love, for aye;
So take me in your arms a space before the east is grey.

When I from hence away am past I shall not find a bride,
And you shall be the first and last I ever lay beside.
She heard and went and knew not why; her heart to his she laid;
Light was the air beneath the sky but dark under the shade.

Oh do you breathe lad, that your breast seems not to rise and fall,
And here upon my bosom prest there beats no heart at all?
Oh lad, what is it lad, that drips wet from your neck and mine?
What is it falling on my lips, my lad that tastes of brine?

Oh like enough, 'tis blood, my dear, for when the knife has slit
The throat across from ear to ear 'twill bleed because of it.
Under the stars the air was light but dark below the boughs,
The still air of the speechless night, when lovers crown their vows.

Goldcup Flowers

Words: A. E. Housman; music: traditional, fitted by Michael Raven

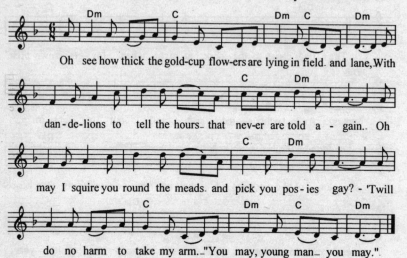

Oh see how thick the gold-cup flow-ers are lying in field and lane, With dan-de-lions to tell the hours that nev-er are told a - gain. Oh may I squire you round the meads and pick you pos-ies gay? - 'Twill do no harm to take my arm. "You may, young man you may."

Ah spring was sent for lass and lad,
'Tis now the blood runs gold,
And man and maid had best be glad
Before the world is old.
What flowers today may flower tomorrow,
But never as good as new.
- Suppose I wound my arm right round -
"Tis true, young man, 'Tis true."

Some lads there are, 'tis shame to say,
That only court to thieve,
And once they bear the bloom away
'Tis little enough they leave.
Then keep your heart for men like me
And safe from trustless chaps.
My love is true and all for you.
"Perhaps, young man, perhaps."

Oh look in my eyes, then, can you doubt?
- Why, 'tis a mile from town.
How green the grass is all about!
We might as well sit down.
- Ah life, what is it but a flower?
Why must true lovers sigh?
Be kind, have pity, my own, my pretty -
"Goodbye, young man, goodbye."

Kiss Me in the Dark

Words: traditional; music: Michael Raven

So here's to ev-ery young man whose fond of a lark,— And here's to ev-ery young maid whose up— to the mark;— And when her lov-er press her she will make this re-mark:— "You may kiss me where you will, my love, but kiss me in the dark.—

Young William was a handsome, a roving sailor boy,
And Sally was the girl he loved, his heart's delight and joy.
He threw his arms around her waist when she made this remark:
"You may kiss me where you will, my love, but kiss me in the dark."

"A captain overhearing these lovers discourse,
He thought that he might kiss the girl and she be none the worse,
He heard young William name the time to meet her in the park;
Says he: "I will go in his stead and kiss her in the dark."

Now the third night after, just at the close of day,
The captain had found out a plan to keep her love away;
With William's dress upon his back he's gone into the park.
He rolled her on the dewy grass and kissed her in the dark.

So in full three months after, to William she was wed,
And in full six months after she safely got her bed.
Her husband he did wonder how it came within the mark,
But little he thought the captain had kissed her in the dark.

The captain stood godfather unto this lovely boy,
And threw him down five hundred pound which he does now enjoy;
And Sally smiles unto herself when thinking of the park,
Where the captain rolled her on the grass and kissed her in the dark.

Jolly Joe the Collier's Son

Words: traditional; chorus by Michael Raven; music: Michael Raven

I'm Jolly Joe the collier's son,
Near Oldbury town I dwell.
I courted lasses many a one,
And loved them all right well;
I courted Nancy and young Kate,
And buxom Nelly too,
But Rachael is the girl I love,
And that you soon shall know.

Come all you colliers in this row,
Who delight in a bonny lass,
Who loves to drink good ale that's brown,
And sparkles in the glass:
My parents they do frown on me,
And say I am to blame,
For keeping Rachael's company,
Who liveth in Mash Lane.

When I rose up one morning,
At the dawning of the day,
I like to hear the small birds sing,
See the lambs to skip and play;
I took a walk to Oldbury town,
Round by the Bilston hill,
And there I spied my own true love,
With Jack of Armlow Mill.

I hid myself behind a shade,
A distance from whence they came;
He gave her kisses one, two, three,
Not knowing I was there:
I boldly stepped up to them,
Saying: "Rogue what hast thou done?
I am Jolly Joe the Collier's son,
So you must either fight or run."

"Hold your hand, dear Joe," she said,
"No more of that let's have,
I'll be thy servant, slave and wife,
Till we both go to one grave."
Then to the church young Rachael went,
Right sore against her will,
So maidens all pity my downfall,
By Jack of Armlow Mill.

Darlaston Dogfight

Words: Tom Langley; music: Michael Raven

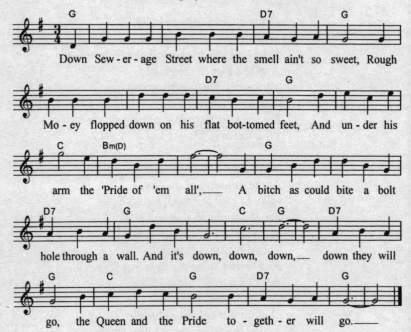

Down Sew-er-age Street where the smell ain't so sweet, Rough Mo-ey flopped down on his flat bot-tomed feet, And un-der his arm the 'Pride of 'em all',— A bitch as could bite a bolt hole through a wall. And it's down, down, down,— down they will go, the Queen and the Pride to-geth-er will go.—

Down Sewerage Street where the smell ain't so sweet,
Ruff Moey flopped down on his flat bottomed feet,
And under his arm the 'Pride of 'Em All,'
The bitch as could bite a bolt hole through a wall.

And back of the Bull Stake by Darlaston Green,
Ben Bates brought his bitch the 'Willenhall Queen',
The Queen had a mouth like a shark with the yaws,
And God help the dog as got stuck in her jaws.

At scratch on the sewer a hundred were stood,
They'd all backed their fancy and thirsted for blood,
They backed with the bookie each bitch at odds on,
No matter who lost he knew he had won.

The lickers licked hard and they licked very well,
They d'aint miss a hair on them dogs - you can tell,
A tot or two more and instead of a dog
They'd have licked all the spikes on a spavined hedgehog.

Old Reuben made referee over the match,
The Pride and the Queen was brought up to scratch.
The bell for the start the timekeeper smote,
And both of them dogs went for each other's throat.

The Queen missed the Pride and Ben Bates shed a tear,
The Pride missed the Queen with a snap you could hear.
Five minutes went by without sign of a bite,
It was more like a dance than a fighting dog fight.

Ruff cussed for a coward the Pride of 'Em All,
The Pride seemed too drunk to be bothered at all.
And as for the Queen, Ben Bates hung his head,
And cried to the crowd to say prayers for the dead.

Then into the pit jumped Ruff Mo with a roar,
He fell on his face and lay flat on the floor,
And then he found out why them dogs wouldn't bite,
Sewer gas in the pit, they was too drugged to fight.

Nailmakers' Strike

Words: traditional; music: Michael Raven

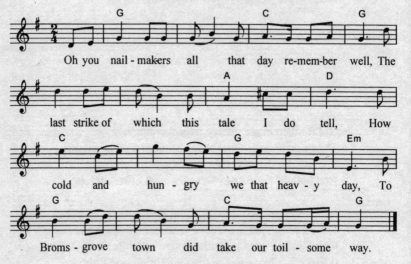

Oh you nail-makers all that day re-mem-ber well, The
last strike of which this tale I do tell, How
cold and hun-gry we that heav-y day, To
Broms-grove town did take our toil-some way.

Oh you nailmakers all that day remember well,
The last strike of which this tale I do tell,
How cold and hungry we that heavy day,
To Bromsgrove town did take our toilsome way.

And these nailforgers, miserable souls,
Will not forget the giver of the coals;
Nailmasters are hard-hearted files,
And the way we took was thirteen long miles.

Oh the slaves abroad in the sugar canes,
Find plenty to help and pity their pains,
But the slaves at home in the mine and fire,
Have plenty to pity, but none to admire.

Oh I wish I could see all nail dealers,
Draw such a load as did we poor nailers,
And to feel such punishment and such smarts,
That it might soften their hard stony hearts.

So as the nailers do suffer such smart,
I hope it will soften old Pharaoh's heart,
And let every nailer tell to his son
The labours that we for our rights have done.

Clemeny

Words: Black Country traditional; music: Michael Raven

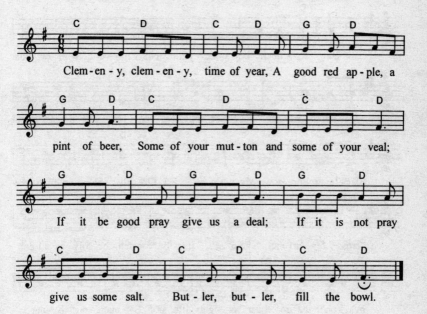

Clem-en-y, clem-en-y, time of year, A good red ap-ple, a
pint of beer, Some of your mut-ton and some of your veal;
If it be good pray give us a deal; If it is not pray
give us some salt. But-ler, but-ler, fill the bowl.

Clemeny, Clemeny, time of year,
A good red apple, a pint of beer,
Some of your mutton and some of your veal;
If it be good pray give us a deal;
If it is not pray give us some salt.
Butler, butler, fill the bowl.

If you fill it of the best,
The Lord'll send your soul to rest;
If you fill it of the small,
Down comes butler, bowl and all.
The bowl is made of good ash tree;
Pray good missus think of me.

One for Peter two for Paul,
Three for him who made us all.
Apple or pear or plum or cherry,
Anything will make us merry;
Off with your kettle and on with your pon,
A good red apple and I'll be gone.

Our Eynuch

Words: from Dr. John Fletcher's collection; music: Michael Raven

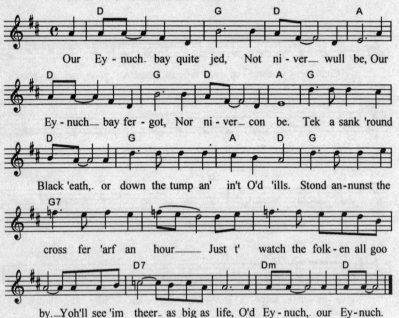

Our Ey - nuch. bay quite jed, Not ni - ver— wull be, Our Ey - nuch— bay fer - got, Nor ni - ver— con be. Tek a sank 'round Black 'eath,. or down the tump an' in't O'd 'ills. Stond an-nunst the cross fer 'arf an hour—— Just t' watch the folk - en all goo by.—Yoh'll see 'im theer- as big as life, O'd Ey - nuch,. our Ey-nuch.

Our Eynuch bay quite jed,
Nor niver wull be,
Our Eynuch bay fergot,
Nor niver con be.
Tek a sank 'round Black'eath,
Or down the tump an' in't o'd 'ills.
Stond annunst the cross fer 'arf-an-hour
Just t' watch the folken all goo by.
Yoh'll see 'im theer as big as life,
O'd Eynuch, our Eynuch.

Our Eynuch left 'is mark,
Yoh can't mistaike et, see?
Is 'ommer prints bin 'ere
An always wull be.
Just look in all the nail shops,
If some bay the'er that meks no odds.
See that ooman scruven up the gledes?
That's 'er wot fashions all the nails,
Yoh'll bet 'er mon bay fer away,
O'd Eynuch, our Eynuch.

Our Eynuch med big chains
(Is ooman med small).
See them th'er big anchors?
Eynuch med 'um all.
In Cradley Heath yoh'll find 'im
Around any chain shop in the day,
Or if it's night look in the pubs
Yoh'll see 'um nustled
        'gainst the cherch
O'd Eynuch, our Eynuch.

No Eynuch bay quite jed,
Nor 'e niver wull be,
O'd Eynuch bay fergot,
Nor niver con be.
'Ast ever sid a Jews 'Arp?
'E med 'um all be Rowley Cherch,
Stond atop Hawes Hill an' look a'dow
See all them lights annunst the cut,
He used to puddle iron th'er
O'd Eynuch, our Eynuch.

Jolly Machine

Words: traditional; music: Michael Raven

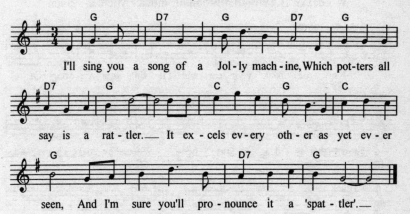

I'll sing you a song of a Jol-ly mach-ine, Which pot-ters all say is a rat-tler.— It ex-cels ev-ery oth-er as yet ev-er seen, And I'm sure you'll pro-nounce it a 'spat-tler'.—

I am quite in earnest so pray lend an ear;
My song it is true and no folly,
As from this machine you have too much to fear;
It's a thief that I call Master Jolly.

A thief did I call it? aye, well you may stare
But prove it I can and most fully;
For if it deprives you of making crock ware
Why, what will become of your belly?

It makes bowls and plates in such mighty big 'rucks';
Believe me, I'm no lying sinner,
And I'm told, by and by, he'll make all our cups;
Then what shall we do for a dinner?

That Jolly's a robber, deny it who can
And brings on distress the most heavy,
But how to avert it I'll tell every man,
Why, down with his half-a-crown levy.

Jolly = Jolley, the man who the man who invented a machine for making crockery ware.
A 'spattler' was a blackleg

Some selfish ones tell us that Jolley won't act;
I think they are greatly mistaken.
It is only to save their half-crown that's a fact
And care not for other men's bacon.

If the fate of the weaver you would avert
And ward off destruction so heavy,
Why come forward like men, that will not be hurt
And pay down your a half-a-crown levy.

Cradley Heath Song

Words: G. B. 'Woodie' Woodall; music: Michael Raven

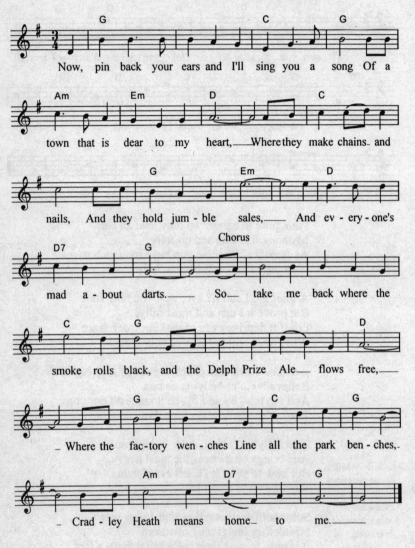

Now, pin back your ears and I'll sing you a song Of a
town that is dear to my heart,—— Where they make chains and
nails, And they hold jum-ble sales,—— And ev-ery-one's
mad a-bout darts.—— So— take me back where the
smoke rolls black, and the Delph Prize Ale— flows free,——
— Where the fac-tory wen-ches Line all the park ben-ches,-
— Crad-ley Heath means home— to me.——

Now, pin back your ears and I'll sing you a song
Of a town that is dear to my heart,
Where they make chains and nails,
And they hold jumble sales,
And everyone's mad about darts.

Chorus:
So take me back where the smoke rolls black,
And the Delph Prize Ale flows free,
Where the factory wenches
Line all the park benches,
Cradley Heath means home to me.

As you walk down each street friendly
    blokes you will meet,
Their faces all full of good cheer.
But their friendship you'll doubt,
When the boozers turn out
And you feel a big fist in your ear.

There's a dim café, with a juke box so gay,
And it's open till late every night;
Where the air sweetly whiffs,
Of last week's fish and chips
And the long-haired boys spoil for a fight.

The gasworks each night, is lit by the light
From the sign of the Collier Inn
Where the old ladies sit,
And stir up the mire
As they lady-like sip their gin.

Now "Ommer 'em Cradley," you can hear
    the crowds roar,
Saturday nights at our speedway track;
And there's many a young bird,
At least so I've heard,
Been 'ommered like hell round the back.

The Boxing Match

Words : traditional; chorus by Michael Raven; music: Michael Raven

Of staunch and firm bot-tom there nev-er was known,— A con-test more wor-thy of fame and re-nown,—Than one fought 'tween Grif-fiths and Bay-lis of late,— For con-quest both bent and for vict'ry e-late, And it's Come, come, come, all ye who list-ens to me,— And nev-er to scorn of the Black Coun-ter-ee.

Of staunch and firm bottom there never was known,
A contest more worthy of fame and renown,
Than one fought 'tween Griffiths and Baylis of late,
For conquest both bent and for vict'ry elate.

And it's come, come, come,
All ye who listens to me,
And never to scorn of the
Black Counteree.

October the fifteenth at one in the day,
Began this most bloody and terrible fray;
Determined they both were on entering the field,
To forfeit their lives before ever they'd yield.

Two hundred and thirteen hard rounds were displayed,
Not one nor the other e'er once seemed afraid;
For more than four hours did the contest prevail,
And vict'ry o'er both still held level her scale.

No shuffling nor tricks, n'er a moment's delay,
Of cowardice once gave the smallest display;
For half minute rests were all the rests given,
To such severe fighting the contest was driven.

The seconds and umpires, unable to say,
On which side the contest the victory lay,
Declared a drawn match as the only sure road,
To stop the two heroes from shedding more blood.

May Birmingham and Wednesb'ry henceforth agree,
And friends their inhabitants evermore be;
When they meet be they social and pleasant inclined,
And give their old grievances all to the wind.

Dudley Canal Tunnel Song

Words: Dudley Tunnel Preservation Society; music: Michael Raven

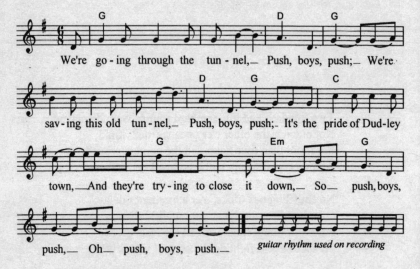

guitar rhythm used on recording

We're going through the tunnel,
Push, boys, push;
We're saving this old tunnel,
Push, boys, push;
It's the pride of Dudley Town,
And they're trying to close it down,
So push boys, push; oh push, boys, push.

We'll go through Castle Mill, Cathedral Arch as well,
There's no more fresh air smell, when you've passed by the Well.

Boats been going through, since 1792,
It's a crime and it's a shame, that we cannot do the same.

Don't let your strength to fail, 'cause we're coming to the jail,
We may get stuck inside, 'cause the boat it is too wide.

The tunnel's two miles long, that's why we sing this song,
It keeps our spirits high, while we cannot see the sky.

We need five thousand pounds, to stop it closing down,
Any money you can pay, may save this Waterway.

And now we're coming nigh, don't you see the sky?
We'll have a celebration, now we've sung it to the nation.

Wedgefield Wake

Words: traditional; chorus by Michael Raven; music: Michael Raven.
The tune for the second half of the verse is the same as for the first

At Wedge-field at one vil-lage_ wake the cock ers all did meet, At Bil-ly Lane's the cock fight-ers to have a spec-ial__ treat. Ri too le roo la roo la roo, ri too la roo la ray, With a click-ing and a clack-ing and a cluck-ing all day, Ho, ho, a clip-wing-red and a span-gled grey.

At Wedgefield at one village wake the cckers all did meet,
At Billy lane's the cockfighters, to have a special treat.
For Charlie Mason's spangled cock was matched to to fight e red,
That came from Willenhall o'er the fields and belonged to Cheeky Ned.

The finer birds in any cock-pit, there never yet was sin,
Though the Wedgefield men declared, their cock was sure to win.
The cocks fought well and feathers flew, all around about the pit,
While blood from both of 'em did flow, yet ne'er un would submit.

At last the spangled Wedgefield bird, began to show defeat,
When Billy Lane he up and swore, the cock should not be beat.
For he would fight the biggest man that came from Wil'n'all town,
When on the word old Cheeky Ned, got up and knocked him down.

To fight they went like two bulldogs, as it is very well known,
Till "Cheeky Ned" seized big Billy's thumb, and bit it into the bone.
At this the Wedgefield men began, their comrade's part to take,
And never was a fiercer fight fought at a village wake.

Collier's Rant

Words: traditional Black Country; music: Michael Raven

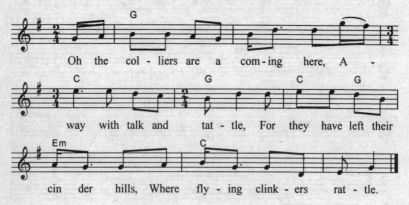

Oh the colliers are coming here,
Away with talk and tattle,
For they have left their cinder hills,
Where flying clinkers rattle.

You've waded once through mud and dirt,
But would you go, I wish to know.

What must be done, what must we do?
Defend yourselves with penny loaves.

So bring your wives and children dear,
For they can sing and bid us cheer.

The constables will form a line,
To face the men from out the mine.

The cavalry must guard the town,
While cinder men go march around.

Away, away, with Tommy Shops,
Long live the King and his fine men.

Hungry Army

Words: traditional; music: Joan Mills

When I was young and in my prime I thought I'd go and join the line, And as a sol-dier cut a shine, And fight in the Hun-gry Ar-my.

Chorus

Sound the bu-gle, blow the horn;— Fight for glor-y night and morn; Hun-gry sol-diers rag-ged and torn Who fight in the Hun-gry Ar-my.

Said the sergeant, "you're just the chap," and placed a knapsack on
my back;
Then sent me off to Ballarat to fight in the hungry army.

Now I went out to drill one day, the wind was rather strong that way.
In fact it blew the lot away that fight in the hungry army.

They cut my hair with a knife and fork, and curled it with a cabbage
stalk.
They sent me off with never a thought to fight in the hungry army.

They sent me out to drill recruits but they kicked me with their
hob-nailed boots.
Oh take, oh take away these brutes that fight in the hungry army.

They gave us soup from an old tin can, a teaspoonful to every man.
I got so fat I couldn't stand to fight in the hungry army.

So now kind friends I must be off; I think I smell the mutton broth,
And here comes General Mowl and Scoff to fight in the hungry army.

Jellon Grame

Words: traditional; music: Michael Raven

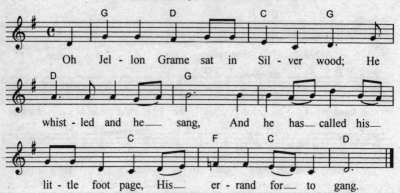

Oh Jellon Grame sat in Silver Wood;
He whistled and he sang,
And he has called his little foot page,
His errand for to gang.

Rise up, my bonny boy, he says,
As quick as e'er you may;
For you must go for Lillie Flower,
Before the break of day.

The boy he's buckled his belt about,
And through the green-wood ran,
And he came to the lady's bower door,
Before the day did dawn.

Ye are bidden come to Silver Wood,
But I fear you'll never come home;
Ye are bidden come to Silver Wood
And speak with Jellon Grame.

She had not ridden a mile, a mile,
A mile but barely three,
Ere she came to a new made grave
Beneath a green oak tree.

Oh then up started Jellon Grame,
Out of a bush nearby;
Light down, light down, now Lillie Flower,
For it's here that you must lie.

She lighted off her milk-white steed,
And knelt upon her knee:
O mercy, mercy, Jellon Grame!
For I'm not prepared to die.

Your bairn that stirs between my sides,
Must shortly see the light,
But to see it weltring in my blood,
Would be a piteous sight.

O should I spare your life he says,
Until that bairn be born?
I know full well your stern father
Would hang me on the morn.

He took no pity on that lady
Though she for life did pray;
But pierced her through the fair body,
As at his feet she lay.

He felt no pity for that lady,
Though she was lying dead;
But he felt some for the bonny boy,
Lay weltring in her blood.

He has taken up that bonny boy,
Called him his sister's son;
He thought no man would e'er find out
The deed that he had done.

But it fell out upon a time,
As a hunting they did go,
That they rested them in Silver Wood
By a stream so sweet did flow.

Then out spake that bonny boy,
Pray tell me Jellon Grame,
The reason that my mother dear,
Does never take me home.

You wonder that your mother dear,
Does never send for thee;
Lo, there's the place I slew thy mother
Beneath that green oak tree.

With that the boy has bent his bow
It was both stout and long,
And through and through him Jellon Grame,
He sent an arrow strong.

Lord Thomas Stuart

Words: traditional Scottish; music: Michael Raven

Thomas Stuart was a lord,
A Lord of mickle land.
He used to wear a coat of gold
But now his grave is green.

Now he has wooed the young countess,
The Countess of Balquhin,
And given her for a morning-gift,
Strathbogie and Aboyne.

But women's wit is aye wilful,
Alas that it ever was so;
She longed to see the morning-gift
That her good lord gave to her.

When steeds were saddled and well bridled,
And ready for to ride,
There came a pain on that good lord,
His back, likewise his side.

He said, "Ride on, my lady fair,
May goodness be your guide,
For I'm so sick and weary that
No farther can I ride."

Now then did come his father dear,
Wearing a golden band;
Says, "Is there no leech in Edinburgh
Can cure my son from wrong?"

"Oh leech is come, and leech is gone,
Yet, father, I'm so worn;
There's not a leech in Edinburgh
Can death from me debar.

"But be a friend to my wife, father,
Restore to her her own;
Restore to her my morning-gift,
Strathbogie and Aboyne.

"It had been good for my wife, father,
To me she'd have born an heir;
He would have got my land and rents,
Where they lie fine and fair."

The steeds they strave into their stables,
The boys couldn't get them bound;
The hounds lay howling on the leash
For their master left behind.

I dreamed a dream since yesterday
I wish it may be good,
That our chamber was full of swine,
And our bed full of blood.

I saw a woman come from the West,
Full sore wringing her hands,
And aye she cried, "Oh and alas,
My good lord's broken bands."

As she came by my good lord's bower,
Saw many black steeds and brown,
"I'm feared it may be many strange lords,
Taking my love from the town."

As she came by my good lord's bower,
Saw many black steeds and grey:
"I'm feared it may be many strange lords,
Taking my lord to the clay."

Poor Law Bill

Words: traditional English; music: Michael Raven

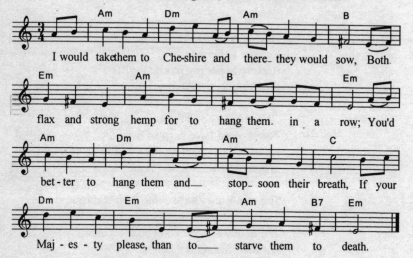

I would take them to Che-shire and there they would sow, Both
flax and strong hemp for to hang them in a row; You'd
bet - ter to hang them and stop soon their breath, If your
Maj - es - ty please, than to starve them to death.

Success to old England, with peace, trade and plenty;
Of good meat abundance, and all kinds of dainty.
Your grain is well housed, with plenty in store,
Yet villains are griping and grinding the poor.

Poor widows may have I may say children three,
To be ta'en from their parents, no daylight to see;
Still more than all this, which will cause grief and strife,
A poor man must be parted from his own loving wife.

O wretched of mortals where this Poor Bill takes place,
Some thousands I fear will soon end your race;
Be put in the grave for to mould and decay,
To rise up in triumph at the last Judgement Day.

There's Campbell and Lord John have plenty of store,
The blood of poor creatures will be placed at their door;
Must be all called aside, no matter how soon,
And swept off the earth with that curs-ed old Brougham.

Now cometh sharp winter when the weather is cold,
How piercing it proves to the infirm and old.
All those who have thousands, they still crave for more;
All you that have plenty, pray think on the poor.

False Love

Words: English traditional; music: Michael Raven

Had I the wings of a snow-white dove, I'd fly across the raging sea Unto some far and distant shore, Where no false love could follow me.

Had I the wings of a snow-white dove,
I'd fly across the raging sea
Unto some far and distant shore,
Where no false love could follow me.

Martinmas wind, when wilt thou blow,
And shake the green leaves off the tree?
O gentle death, when wilt thou come?
For of my life I am weary.

'Tis not the frost that freezes fell,
Nor winter's snow that beats the lea;
'Tis not such cold that makes me cry,
But my love's heart grown cold to me.

When we came in by London town
We were a comely sight to see;
My love was clad in the black velvet,
And I myself in cramasie.

But had I thought, before I kissed,
That love had been so ill to win,
I'd locked my heart in a case of gold
And pinned it with a silver pin.

Now Arthur-Seat shall be my bed,
And sheets of silk no more for me;
Saint Anton's well shall be my drink,
Since my true-love's forsaken me.

The Trooper's Horse

Words: traditional; music: Michael Raven

It's a land-la-dy's daugh-ter, ve-ry meek and mild, And its

green, oh— green, the— leaves they do grow, And—

she— took— sick and to her bed con-fined, And it's

oh— young— man— do you tell me so? It

was— a bold troop-er who— rode up to the inn, And it's

green, oh— green, the— leaves they do grow, He's—

cold and tired and hun-gry and wet un-to his skin, And it's

oh— young man— do you tell me so?

It's a landlady's daughter, very meek and mild,
And it's green, oh green, the leaves they do grow;;
And she took sick and to her bed confined,
And it's oh young man do you tell me so?
It was a bold trooper who rode up to the inn,
And it's green, oh green, the leaves they do grow;
He's cold and tired and hungry and wet unto his skin,
And it's, oh young man, do you tell me so?

The landlady put them in bed together,
And it's green, oh green, the leaves they do grow;
To see if one couldn't cure the other,
And it's oh young man do you tell me so?
Oh what is this here, and what is it called?
And it's green, oh green, the leaves they do grow;
It's my fine trusty nag and they call him bald,
And it's, oh young man, do you tell me so?

Oh what is this here, and what is it called?
And it's green, oh green, the leaves they do grow;
It's my little well where you can water old bald,
And it's oh young man do you tell me so?
Suppose that my nag he should slip in?
And it's green, oh green, the leaves they do grow;
Just catch on the grass that grows around the brim,
And it's, oh young man, do you tell me so?

How can you tell if he's had his fill?
And it's green, oh green, the leaves they do grow;
He'll hang down his head, and turn from the well,
And it's oh young man do you tell me so?
How can I tell when your old nag wants more?
And it's green, oh green, the leaves they do grow;
He'll rear up his head and go pawing at the door,
And it's, oh young man, do you tell me so?

Young Johnstone

Words: traditional, taken from several sources and anglicized
by Michael Raven; music: Michael Raven

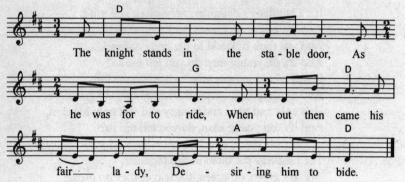

The knight stands in the sta-ble door, As
he was for to ride, When out then came his
fair la-dy, De-sir-ing him to bide.

The knight stands in the stable door,
As he was for to ride,
When out then came his fair lady,
Desiring him to bide.

How can I bide? how dare I bide?
How can I bide with thee?
Have I not killed thine own brother,
Thou hadst not more than he.

If you have killed my own brother,
Alas, and woe is me!
But if I save your fair body,
The better you'll like me.

She's taken him to her secret bower,
Locked with a silver pin,
And she's up to her highest tower,
To watch that none come in.

She had not long gone up the stair,
And entered in her tower,
When four and twenty armed knights
Came riding to the door.

Now God you save, my fair lady,
I pray you tell to me,
Saw you not a wounded knight
Come riding by this way?

Yes, bloody, bloody was his sword,
And bloody were his hands;
But if the steed he rides be good,
He's past fair Scotland's strands.

Light down, light down then, gentlemen,
And take some bread and wine;
The better you will him pursue
When you shall lightly dine.

We thank you for your bread, lady;
We thank you for your wine.
I'd give thrice three thousand pounds
Your fair body was mine.

Then she's gone to her secret bower,
Her husband dear to meet;
But he drew out his bloody sword,
And wounded her so deep.

What aileth thee now, my good lord?
What aileth thee at me?
Have you not got my father's gold,
But and my mother's fee?

Now live, now live, my fair lady;
O live but half an hour.
There's never a leech in fair Scotland
But shall be at thy bower.

How can I live? how shall I live?
How can I live for thee?
See you not where my red heart's blood
Runs trickling down my knee?

Take thy harp into thy hand,
And harp out over yon plain,
And ne'er think more on thy true-love
Than if she had never been.

He had not long been from that house,
And on his saddle set,
Till four and twenty broad arrows
Were thrilling in his heart.

The Backwoodsman

Words: traditional; music: Michael Raven

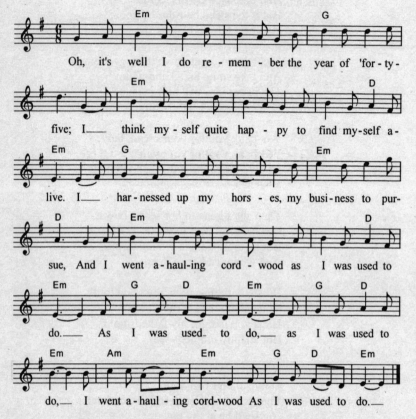

Oh, it's well I do re-mem-ber the year of 'for-ty-five; I— think my-self quite hap-py to find my-self a-live. I— har-nessed up my hors-es, my busi-ness to pur-sue, And I went a-haul-ing cord-wood as I was used to do.— As I was used- to do,— as I was used to do,— I went a-haul-ing cord-wood As I was used to do.—

Oh, it's well I do remember the year of 'forty-five;
I think myself quite happy to find myself alive.
I harnessed up my horses, my business to pursue,
And I went a-hauling cordwood as I was used to do.

Now I only hauled one load where I should have hauled four;
I went down to Omemee and I could haul no more.
The taverns being open, good liquor flowing free,
And I hadn't emptied one glass when another was filled for me.

Now I met an old acquaintance, and I dare not tell his name;
He was going to a dance and I thought I'd do the same.
He was going to a dance where the fiddle sweetly played,
And the boys and girls all danced till the breaking of the day.

So I puts me saddle on my arm and started for the barn,
To saddle up old gray nag, not thinking any harm.
I saddled up old gray nag, and I rode away so still,
And I never drew a long breath till I came to Downeyville.

So when I got to Downeyville the night was far advanced;
I got upon the floor for to have a little dance.
The fiddler being rested, his arm both stout and strong,
He played the reels of old Ireland for four hours long.

Kate of Coalbrook Dale

Words: traditional; music: Michael Raven

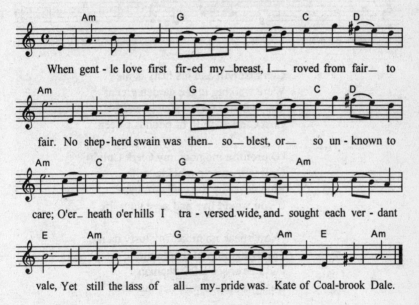

When gent-le love first fir-ed my breast, I roved from fair to fair. No shep-herd swain was then so blest, or so un-known to care; O'er heath o'er hills I tra-versed wide, and sought each ver-dant vale, Yet still the lass of all my pride was Kate of Coal-brook Dale.

How happy, sure were then my days, such tranquil joys I knew;
Where'er I went I spoke her praise, I found her just and true;
For oft in yonder shady grove, I told my ardent tale,
And whispered themes of softest love to Kate of Coalbrook Dale.

But ah! how fleeting was my bliss, for I'd no wealth in store;
Her parents thought our love amiss, we part to meet no more;
But hope shall cheer my tortured mind, for what will tears avail,
Though thou wert faithful, fair and kind, dear Kate of Coalbrook Dale?

Clerk Colvill

Words: English traditional; music: Michael Raven

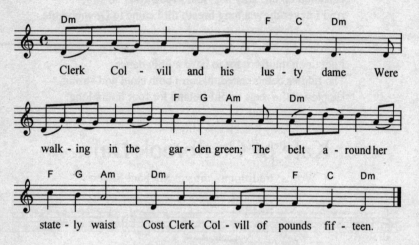

Clerk Col - vill and his lus - ty dame Were walk - ing in the gar - den green; The belt a - round her state - ly waist Cost Clerk Col - vill of pounds fif - teen.

Clerk Colvill and his lusty dame
Were walking in the garden green;
The belt around her stately waist
Cost Clerk Colvill of pounds fifteen.

"O promise me now, my Clerk Colvill,
Or it will cost ye muckle strife,
Ride never by the wells of Slane
If you would live and save your life."

"Now speak no more, my lusty dame,
Speak no more of that to me;
Did I ne'er see a fair woman
But I would sin with her fair body?"

"Wash on, wash on, my bonny maid,
And wash so clean your sark of silk;"
"And well fare you, fair gentleman,
Your body whiter than the milk."

He's taken leave of his gay lady,
Not minding what his lady said,
And he's rode by the wells of Slane,
Where washing was a bonny maid.

He's taken her by her milk-white hand
And likewise by the grass green sleeve,
And laid her down upon the green
And he's forgotten his gay lady.

Then loud, loud cried the Clerk Colvill,
"O my head it pains me sair;"
"Then take, then take" the maiden said,
"And from my sark you'll cut a gare."

Then she's given him a little bone knife
And from her sark he cut a share;
She's tied it round his whey-white face
But oh his head it ached mair.

Then louder cried the Clerk Colvill,
"O sairer, sairer aches my head;"
"And sairer, sairer e'er will be"
The maiden cries, "till you be dead."

Out then he drew his shining blade,
Thinking to stick her where she stood,
But she was vanished to a fish
And swam far off, a fair mermaid.

"O mother, O mother braid my hair;
My lusty lady, make my bed;
O brother take my sword and spear,
For I have seen the false mermaid."

Clerk, or Clark or Clarke, is derived
from 'cleric' but was used as the title
of a knight at arms, probably
because he took religious vows.

Childe Owlet

Words: traditional; music: Michael Raven

La - dy Ers-kine sits in her cham - ber Sew-ing her sil-ken— seam, A— cloak of gold for Childe Ow - let As he goes out— and in, As he goes out— and in.

Lady Erskine sits in her chamber
Sewing her silken seam,
A cloak of gold for Childe Owlet
As he goes out and in.

But it fell once upon a day
She unto him did say:
"Ye must cuckold Lord Ronald
For all his lands and ley."

"Oh cease! Forbid, madam" he says,
"That this should e'er be done!
How would I cuckold Lord Ronald
And me his sister's son?"

Then she's ta'en out a little penknife
That lay below her bed,
Put it below her green stay's cord
Which made her body bleed.

Then in it came him Lord Ronald
Hearing his lady's moan;
"What blood is this, my dear" he says,
"That sparks on the fire stone?"

"Young Childe Owlet, your sister's son
Is now gone from my bower;
If I had not been a good woman
I'd have been Childe Owlet's whore."

Then he has ta'en him Childe Owlet,
Laid him in prison strong,
And all his men a council held
How they would work him wrong.

Some said they would Childe Owlet hang,
Some said they would him burn;
Some said they would have Childe Owlet
Between wild horses torn.

"There are horses in your stables stand
Can run right speedily,
And ye will to your stable go
And wile out four for me."

They put a foal to either foot
And one to either hand,
And sent them down to Darlingmuir
As fast as they could gang.

There was not a stick in Darlingmuir
Nor any piece o' rush,
But dropped on it Childe Owlet's blood
And pieces of his flesh.

There was not a stick in Darlingmuir,
Nor any piece o' rind
But dropped on it Childe Owlet's blood,
And pieces of his skin.

Bonny Hind

Words: English traditional; music: Michael Raven

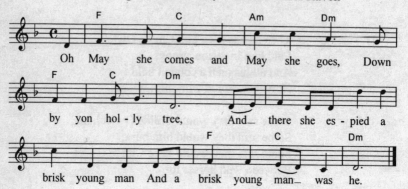

Oh May she comes and May she goes,
Down by yon holly tree,
And there she espied a brisk young man
And a brisk young man was he.

Give me your mantle green fair maid,
Give me your maidenhead,
And he has lain her down and a-down,
The green grass for a bed.

Perhaps there may be a child, kind sir,
Perhaps there may be none,
But if you be a gentleman
You'll tell to me your name.

I am no gentleman fair maid,
But new come from the sea;
And when I'm in my father's house,
John Randall they call me.

You lie, you lie my bonny boy,
So loud I hear you lie;
For I am Lord Randall's only daughter,
He has no more but me.

You lie, you lie, my bonny maid,
So loud I hear you lie;
For I am Lord Randall's only son,
Just now come o'er the sea.

She's put her hand down by her gown,
And she's ta'en out a knife,
And then let flow her own heart's blood,
And ta'en away her life.

And he's ta'en up his bonny sister,
With the salt tear in his eye;
And he has buried his bonny sister
Beneath the holly tree.

And then he's ran him o'er the dale,
His father dear to see.
"Sing oh and oh for the bonny hind
Beneath yon holly tree".

"What needs you care for your bonny hind?
For it you need not care.
For there's many many more in yonder park,
And five score hinds to spare."

"I care not for your hind my lord,
I care not for your fee;
But oh and oh for my bonny hind,
Beneath yon holly tree."

"Oh were you at your sister's bower,
Your sister fair to see;
You'll think no more of your bonny hind
Beneath yon holly tree."

Lady Helen

Words: traditional, collated and abridged from several sources;
music: Michael Raven

There lived a lord on yon— sea - side, And he thought up - on— a while,— How— he would go o'er the— salt— sea A— la - dy— to— be— guile.

18.6.1999

There lived a Lord on yon seaside,
And he thought upon a while,
How he would go o'er the salt sea
A lady to beguile.

O make your bed Fair Helen, he said,
And learn to lie on it alone,
For I am going o'er the salt sea
A bright bride to bring home.

How can I make my bed, she says,
Unless I make it oh so wide,
When I have seven of your sons
To lie down by my side?

Oh who will bake my bridal bread,
And brew of your bridal ale?
And I will welcome your gay lady
That you bring o'er the dale.

It's I will bake your bridal bread
And brew of your bridal ale,
And I will welcome your gay lady
That you bring o'er the dale

She's ta'en her young son in her arms,
And another in her hand,
And she's up to the highest tower
To see him come to land.

You're welcome home my gay lady,
Ay, a welcome here waits thee,
And welcome home, my Lord she said
Though tears did blind her ee.

When day was gone and night come on
And ev'ry man was bound to bed;
The bridegroom and the bonny bride
In their chamber were laid.

Helen made her bed a little forbye,
To hear what bride and groom might say
And ever alas! Fair Helen, she cried
That I should see this day!

Oh if my sons were seven grey rats,
And run they on the castle wall,
Then I a grey cat would soon become
And soon would kill them all.

Helen made her bed a little forbye,
To hear what bride and groom might say;
And ever alas! Fair Helen, she cried
That I should see this day!

Oh if my sons were seven grey rats,
And run they on the castle wall,
Then I a grey cat would soon become
And soon would kill them all.

Oh if my sons were seven young hares,
Running o'er yon hilly lee,
Then I a greyhound would soon become
And worried they should be.

And then up spoke the bonny bride
In the chamber where she lay:
There is a lady in this house
She will go mad come day.

She's up and gone to Helen's bed;
What ails you to make such moan?
And tell to me your father's name,
And from whence you did come.

King Henry was my father dear,
Queen Catherine she was my mother,
Lady Anne was my sister
And Frederick my brother.

And when I was six years of age,
A knight stole me from my father's hall,
And took me far across the sea
Unto this cursed shore.

Then up spoke the bonny bride,
By her Lord there as she lay:
Lie down, lie down, my dear sister,
There's no ill done for me.

O seven ships conveyed me here,
Seven ships came o'er the main;
And four of them shall stay with you,
And three convey me home.

Though when I'm home to my father's house
They will laugh at me and scorn,
To go away a wedded wife
Come home a maid as born.

Soldier's Fancy

Words: traditional; music: traditional, fitted and adapted
by Michael Raven

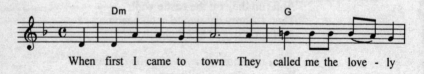

When first I came to town They called me the love - ly

Nan - cy, But___ now they've changed my___

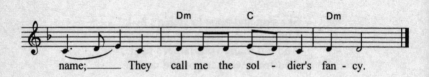

name;___ They call me the sol - dier's fan - cy.

When first I came to town
They called me the lovely Nancy,
But now they've changed my name;
They call me the soldier's fancy.

My fancy lad's in Quod
But I am free and willing,
To turn out of a night
To gain an honest shilling.

And when my love comes home,
We will roll in riches,
And I will buy my love
A pair of buckskin breeches.

A coat I'll buy my love
With silver buttons to it,
And I will let them know
I am the girl can do it.

Michael Turner's Epitaph

Words: anonymous; music: Michael Raven

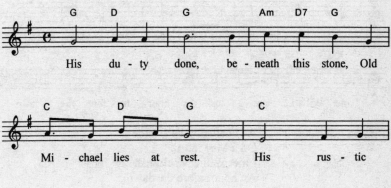

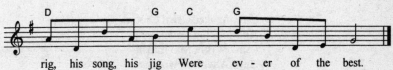

24.5.1999

His duty done, beneath this stone,
Old Michael lies at rest.
His rustic rig, his song, his jig
Were ever of the best.

With nodding head the choir he led,
That none should start too soon.
The seconds, too, he sang full true;
His viol played the tune.

And when at last his age had passed
One hundred - less eleven,
With faithful cling to fiddle string
He sang himself to Heaven.

This poem is engraved on the tombstone of
Michael Turner (1796-1885), bootmaker,
parish clerk and fiddler of
Wareham, Sussex.

Burning of Auchindown

Words: traditional Scottish; music: Michael Raven

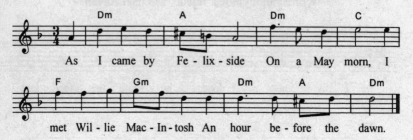

As I came by Felix-side
On a May morn,
I met Willie MacIntosh
An hour before the dawn.

Coming o'er Cairn Croom,
And looking down, man,
I saw Willie MacIntosh
Burn Auchindown, man.

Head me or hang me,
That cannot fright me;
I'll burn Auchindown,
Ere the life leave me.

Coming down Deeside,
In a clear morning,
Auchindown was in flame,
Ere the cock-crowing.

Turn, Willie MacIntosh,
Turn, I bid you;
Would you burn Auchindown?
Huntly will head you.

Bonny Willie MacIntosh,
Where left you your men?
I left them in the Stapler,
But they'll never come home again.

Bonny Willie MacIntosh,
Where now are your men?
I left them in the Stapler,
Sleeping in their sheen.

My Last Farewell to Stirling

Words: traditional Australian; music: Michael Raven

No lark in trans - port_ mounts the_ sky, Nor leaves with

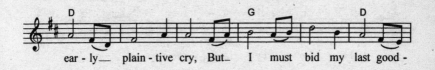

ear - ly_ plain - tive cry, But_ I must bid my last good -

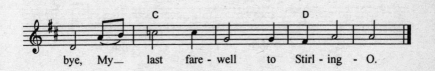

bye, My_ last fare - well to Stirl - ing - O.

No lark in transport mounts the sky,
Nor leaves with early plaintive cry,
But I must bid my last goodbye,
My last farewell to Stirling-O.

No more I'll wander through the glen
To rob the roost o' the pheasant hen,
Nor chase the rabbits to their den
When I am far from Stirling-O.

Now fare you well, my dearest dear;
For you I'll shed a bitter tear,
But you may find some other dear
When I am far from Stirling-O.

Now fare you well, for I am bound
For twenty years to Van Diemen's Land,
But speak of me and of what I have done
When I am far from Stirling-O.

Bold Fisherman

Words: traditional; music: Michael Raven
A lover returned? Or Jesus taking her to a nunnery to wed with God?

As I walked out one May— morn - ing, Down by the ri - ver - si - de, And— there I saw a fish - er - man Come row - ing— down— the tide.

"Good morning to you,
    fisherman,
Good morning, Sir, I pray,
A welcome to you fisherman
Just by the break of day."

Then he rowed his boat unto
    the shore
And tied it to a stake.
He stepped up to this
    gay lady
And hold of her did take.

And he pulled off his morning
    gown
And spread it on the ground;
And there she saw three chins
    of gold
All from his neck hung down.

Down on her bended knees
    did fall:
"Oh, pardon, Sir, on me
For calling you a fisherman,
Come rowing on the sea."

"Rise up, rise up, my pretty
    maid,
And come along with me.
There's not one word that
    you have said
The least offended me.

"I'll take you to your father's
    house
And married we shall be;
And you shall have a
    fisherman
To row you on the sea."

Can y Melinydd

Words: *Song of the Miller*, Welsh, translated, and Michael Raven;
music: traditional, arranged and adapted by Michael Raven

I have a gol - den po - ny,— The fleet - est ev - er seen,—Whose fly - ing feet are shod, love, with shoes of sil - ver sheen.. Fal dee ral lal dee ri dee row, Fal dee ral lal dee ri dee row Fal dee ral dee ri dee row— oh— oh— oh— oh— oh— oh,— Ah— ah— ah— ah— ah— ah— ah dee ri dee row..

Twelve pullets and a cockerel,
A score of brindled kine,
And fatter pigs than any -
Were never pigs like mine.

Off goes my filly flying
On flashing silver shoon
O'er river, field and mountain
To bring you back the moon.

I'll travel through the valleys;
I'll travel through the hills;
I'll travel through the forests;
I'll go where e'er you will.

Brave Collier Lads

Words: traditional; music: traditional, fitted by Michael Raven

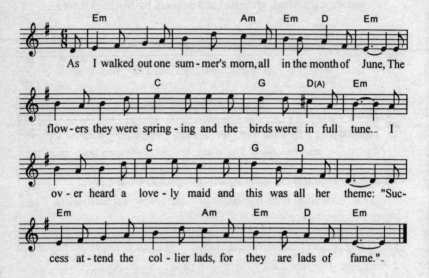

As I walked out one summer's morn, all in the month of June, The flowers they were springing and the birds were in full tune. I overheard a lovely maid and this was all her theme: "Success attend the collier lads, for they are lads of fame."

I stepped up to her and bending on my knee
I asked her pardon for making with her so free:
"My pardon is granted, young collier" she replies;
"Pray do you belong to the brave Union boys?"

"You may say I'm a collier as black as a sloe;
And all night long I am working down below."
"Oh I do love a collier as I do love my life -
My father was a pitman all the days of his life."

"Come now my young collier and rest here awhile,
And when I've done milking, I'll give you a smile."
He kissed her sweet lips while milking her cow;
And the lambs they were sporting all in the morning dew.

"Come all you noble gentlemen, wherever you may be;
Do not pull down their wages, nor break their unity.
You see they hold like brothers, like sailors on the sea;
They do their best endeavours for their wives and family."

Then she clapt her arms around him, like Venus round the vine;
"You are my jolly collier lad, you've won this heart of mine,
And if that you do win the day, as you have won my heart,
I'll crown you with honour and forever take your part."

Tommy Note

Words: traditional; music: traditional, fitted by Michael Raven.
Repeat the tune for 2nd half of verse and chorus adapting as required

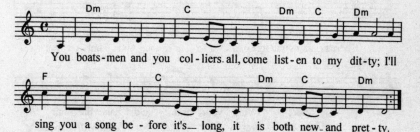

You boats-men and you col-liers. all, come list-en to my dit-ty; I'll
sing you a song be - fore it's__ long, it   is both new_ and pret-ty.

You boatsmen and you colliers all, come listen to my ditty;
I'll sing you a song before it's long, it is both new and pretty.
It is concerning Tommy Shops, and the high field ruffian;
He pays you with a Tommy Note, you must have that or nothing.

To my ral to my ral, to my ridee-o, to my ral to my ridee-ay,
To my ral to my ral, to my ridee-o, hey ho the Tommy-o.

With the colliers I begin, how they pay each other;
Nothing have they but a Tommy Note from one week to the other.
On Saturday when a week's work is done and to receive their money,
The high field devil has learned a trick, to pay them off with Tommy.

And now the boatsmen I bring in that sails high field to Runcan;
Likewise the boatsmen and their wives, they curse him at the junction.
When they had done their Runcan voyage and go to receive their money,
One half stops for hay and corn, the other half for Tommy.

Then to the Tommy Shops we go to fetch our week's provisions;
Their oatmeal, sugar, salt and soap, short weight and little measure.
If we had money instead of this, provisions we'd have plenty;
The profit they get out of us is nine shillings out of twenty.

There is one amongst the rest that knows the art of boating;
He vows and swears a wife he'll have, so long he has gone a-courting.
He vows he will married be, come listen to the joke, Sir,
And when the parson's done his work, pay him with a Tommy Note, Sir.

Stafford County Fair

Words: Michael Raven; music: With Jockey to the Fair

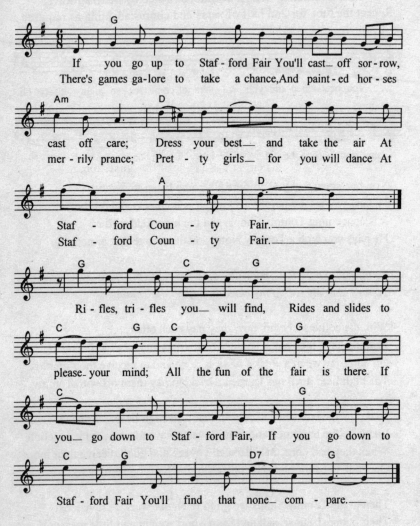

If you go up to Stafford Fair
You'll cast off sorrow, cast off care;
Dress your best and take the air
At Stafford County Fair.
There's games galore to take a chance,
And painted horses merrily prance;
Pretty girls for you will dance
At Stafford County Fair.

Chorus:
Rifles, trifles you will find,
Rides and slides to please your mind;
All the fun of the fair is there
If you go down to Stafford Fair,
If you go down to Stafford Fair
You'll find that none compare.

There's cows and yows all in a row,
And they all cut the finest show;
Prizes to the best will go
At Stafford County Fair.
There's hogs and dogs and horses too,
And tractors and machines so new
Bringing the Harvest Home to you,
At Stafford County Fair.

There's beer to drink and barley wine,
And there they have no closing time;
We can promise the sun will shine
At Stafford County Fair.
There's tinkers, tailors, soldiers, spies;
The truth of that no one denies.
There half of the world goes by
At Stafford County Fair.

There's music there both night and day,
And every tune is bright and gay;
Played to drive your cares away
At Stafford County Fair.
You'll see old Jack out there to beg,
A-hobbling on his wooden leg,
All in his uniform of red
At Stafford County Fair.

One day the Bishop went to see
The cause of this frivolity,
But his wrath soon turned to glee
At Stafford County Fair.
There's gambling men and gay young girls
With golden hair and quivering curls;
Overhead the Big Wheel whirls
At Stafford County Fair.

Redditch Needlemakers' Lament

Words: traditional; music: traditional, fitted by Michael Raven

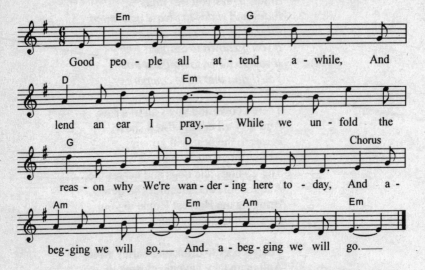

Good people all attend awhile,
And lend an ear I pray,
While we unfold the reason why
We're wandering here today.

It is because we're out of work,
And bread we can't procure;
To see our children pine for food,
What parents can e'er endure?

What parents can behold a child
With tears in either eye?
Petition for a little bread,
Which, ah! he must deny.

And when the morning light
 appears
Our children round us fly.
Regardless of our nightly grief
To us for bread they cry.

They cry to us with meagre
 looks,
Which makes our hearts to ache;
Then unto us a trifle give
For these poor children's sake.

Our visit now to you, kind friends,
We hope you will excuse;
And now we have explained our
 case
We trust you'll not refuse.

A mite from you, though e'er so
 small,
Will greatly us befriend;
We hope you will no poorer be,
But richer in the end.

For he that giveth to the poor
But lendeth to the the Lord;
So now, kind friends, on us bestow,
What e're you can afford.

And what on us you now bestow
We'll thankfully receive,
And hope you will a pleasure feel,
That you did us relieve.

Rewarded with a hundred-fold,
While here on earth you stay;
And after death you may enjoy
An everlasting day.

Pioneers' Song

Words: traditional; music: traditional, fitted by Michael Raven

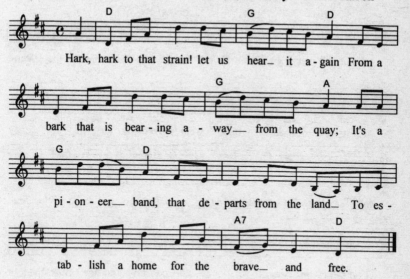

Hark, hark to that strain! let us hear— it a-gain From a
bark that is bear-ing a-way— from the quay; It's a
pi-on-eer— band, that de-parts from the land— To es-
tab-lish a home for the brave— and free.

"Farewell" sing the crew as they sail from our view,
"The land of the paupers is not for the free;
We sail for the West where the weary shall rest
And the Bastile of England no more shall we see."

The tyrants of state in their pride and their hate,
Have driven their thousands to premature graves;
The lives of the poor, they think of no more -
Far less than the Planters would think of their slaves.

"Farewell and away o'er the bright bounding spray"
Sing the bold pioneers as they dash o'er the wave;
"There's a health in the gale as it fills every sail
And bears us away to the home of the brave."

The dear friends we leave, for them we may grieve,
And may offer a tribute to memory dear;
For the sorrow and care they are all doomed to bear
Will forever call forth to our eyelids a tear.

But away with the pain, we shall see them again;
We are only preparing a way for the rest.
Then blow breezes blow, as onward we go;
The Potters shall yet have a home in the West!

Sarah Collins

Words: traditional; music: traditional, fitted by Michael Raven

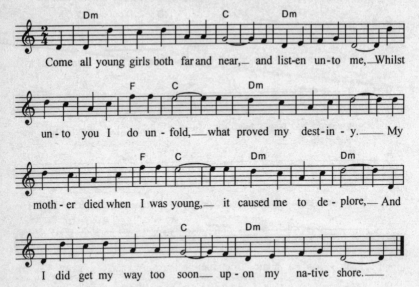

Come all young girls both far and near,— and list-en un-to me,—Whilst un-to you I do un-fold,—what proved my dest-in-y.—— My moth-er died when I was young,— it caused me to de-plore,—And I did get my way too soon—— up-on my na-tive shore.——

Sarah Collins is my name, most dreadful is my fate.
My father reared me tenderly, the truth I do relate,
But I did take bad company along with many more,
It led to my discovery upon my native shore.

My trial it approached fast, before the Judge I stood;
And when the Judge his sentence passed, it fairly chilled my blood.
Crying: "You must be transported for fourteen years or more
And go from hence across the seas, unto Van Dieman's shore."

The sea was rough, ran mountains high, with us poor girls 'twas hard;
No friend but God to us came nigh, no one did us regard.
At length alas we reached the land, it grieved us ten times more,
That wretched place, Van Dieman's Land, far from our native shore.

They bound us two by two in chains, and whipped and lashed along;
They marched us in the burning sun, our days both hard and long.
We often wished, when we lay down, we may never rise no more,
To meet our savage governors upon Van Dieman's shore.

Come all young girls and maidens fair, bad company forsake;
If tongue can tell our overthrow, it would make your hearts to ache.
You girls, I pray, be ruled me, your wicked ways give o'er,
For fear like us you spend your days upon Van Dieman's shore.

Tiffany Street

Words: Michael Raven; music: traditional, arranged Michael Raven

2.8.1999

As I was a walking down Tiffany Street
One evening in August I chanced there to meet
A sailor just home from the dark rolling sea,
And all his appearance with me did agree.

He asked me my name and from whence I came,
And told me fine tales of the wars out in Spain,
And how he was wounded off High Barbary,
And spent half his life in just searching for me.

The wine it flowed fast and the wine it flowed free,
And never had maiden such fine company;
We walked by the shore 'neath a bright Summer moon,
And what came to pass came never too soon.

By daylight he'd gone, left me all lone,
But not broken-hearted, in truth, I do own,
And when I am low and my heart it be sad,
I smile when I think of that bonny brave lad.

Young Redin

Words: traditional, anglicized, abridged and adapted by
Michael Raven; music: traditional/Michael Raven

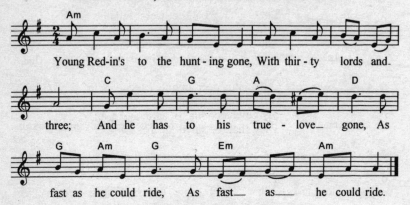

Young Redin's to the hunting gone,
With thirty lords and three;
And he has to his true-love gone,
As fast as he could ride.

You're welcome here, my young Redin,
For coal and candle-light;
And so are you, my young Redin,
To bide with me this night.

I thank you for your light, lady,
So do I for your coal;
But thrice as fair a lady as thee
Meets me at Brandie's well.

When they were at their supper set,
Merrily drinking wine,
This lady has ta'en a sore sickness,
And to her bed has gone.

Young Redin he has followed her,
A sadly man was he;
He found his true-love in her bower,
The tear was in her eye.

When he was in her arms laid,
Giving her kisses sweet,
Then out she's ta'en a little penknife,
And wounded him so deep.

O long, long, is the winter night,
And slowly dawns the day;
There is a slain knight in my bower,
I wish he were away.

Then up spoke her bower-woman,
And she spoke all with spite -
There be a slain knight in your bower,
It's you that has the wight.

O heal this deed on me, Meggy,
O heal this deed on me,
My gowns of silk, of satin and gold,
They shall be sewn for thee.

They've booted him, and they've spurred him,
As he was wont to ride:-
And the dreary grave they gave him
Was the waters of the Clyde.

O there came a seeking young Redin,
Many a lord and knight;
And there came a seeking young Redin
Many a lady bright.

They've sought Clyde's water up and down,
They've sought it out and in,
And the deepest place of Clyde's water
They found young Redin in.

O white, white, were his wounds washed,
As white as a linen clout;
But as the traitor she came near,
His wounds they bled out!

It's surely been my bower-woman,
The lady loudly cried:
I'd ne'er have slain him young Redin
And thrown him in the Clyde.

Then they've made a big bonfire,
The bower-woman to burn;
But it took only the cruel hands
That put young Redin in.

Then they've ta'en out the bower-woman,
And put the lady in;
But it took only the false, false arms,
That young Redin lay in.

Jolly Highwayman

Words: traditional; music: traditional, fitted and adapted by Michael
Raven. Drone on notes G and D throughout

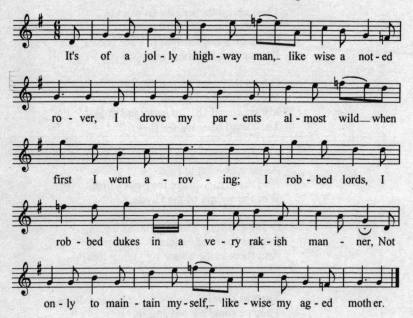

It's of a jolly highwayman, likewise a noted rover;
I drove my parents almost wild when first I went a-roving.
I robbed lords, I robbed dukes in a very rakish manner,
Not only to maintain myself, likewise my aged mother.

The very first man that I did rob, it being a lord of honour,
I did abuse that mighty lord in a very rakish manner.
"Deliver your money, my lord," said I, "without any more desire,
For if you don't it's my desire with powder and shot to fire."

I put a pistol to his breast, which made him for to shiver;
Ten thousand guineas all in bright gold to me he did deliver,
Besides a gold repeater watch to me he did surrender;
I thought I had a noble prize to add unto my plunder.

The very next man that I did rob was down in Kelpin's Garden,
And not long after he was robbed, in Newgate I was fastened.
To hear the turnkey's locks and bolts at six o'clock in the morning,
Glad was I, resolved to die, so fare you well, companions.

Demon Lover

Words: traditional; music: traditional, fitted by Michael Raven

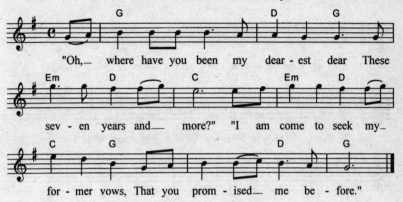

"Oh,— where have you been my dear-est dear These sev-en years and— more?" "I am come to seek my— for-mer vows, That you prom-ised— me be-fore."

"Oh, where have you been my dearest dear
These seven years and more?"
"I am come to seek my former vows,
That you promised me before."

"Away with your former vows," she says,
"Or else you will breed strife;
Away with your former vows," she says,
"For I'm become a wife."

"I am married to a ship-carpenter,
A ship-carpenter he's bound;
I wouldn't he knew my mind this night
For twice five hundred pound."

She has put her foot on good ship-board,
And on ship-board she's gone,
And the veil that hung over her face
Like gold shone thereupon.

She had not sailed a league, a league,
A league but barely two,
Till she did mind on the husband she left,
And her wee young son also.

"Oh, hold your tongue, my dearest dear,
Away with all your fears;
I'll show you where the white lilies grow
In the bottom of the sea."

John Whitehouse

Words: traditional; music: traditional, fitted by Michael Raven

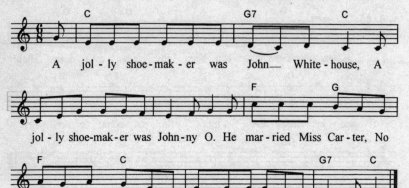

A jol-ly shoe-mak-er was John— White-house, A jol-ly shoe-mak-er was John-ny O. He mar-ried Miss Car-ter, No dam-sel looked smart-er, But he'd caught a tart-ar had John-ny O.

A jolly shoemaker was John Whitehouse,
A jolly shoemaker was Johnny O.
He married Miss Carter,
No damsel looked smarter,
But he'd caught a tartar
Had Johnny O.

He tied a rope round her did John Whitehouse,
He tied a rope round her did Johnny O.
To escape from hot water
To Smithfield he brought her,
But nobody bought her
From Johnny O.

"Oh who wants a wife," says John Whitehouse,
"A sweet pretty wife, " says Johnny O,
But somehow they tell us
Those wife-dealin' fellers
Were all of them sellers
Poor Johnny O.

The rope it was ready for John Whitehouse,
"Come give me the rope," says Johnny O.
"I won't stand to wrangle,
Myself I will strangle
And hang dingle dangle,"
Says Johnny O.

Lord Paget

Words and music traditional, arranged and adapted by Michael Raven

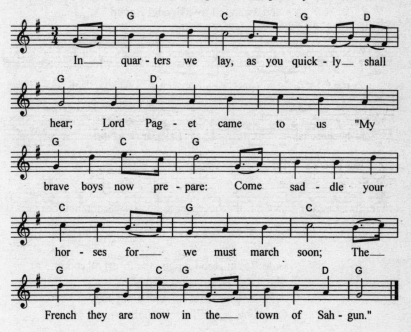

In— quar - ters we lay, as you quick - ly— shall hear; Lord Pag - et came to us "My brave boys now pre - pare: Come sad - dle your hor - ses for— we must march soon; The— French they are now in the— town of Sah - gun."

We travelled all night until day it did break,
When eight of those French dogs near a bridge we did take;
But two of them got back to the town of Sahgun, (Sargoon)
And informed the French army that the English were come.

Then they formed themselves close and the fray it began;
They thought to dismount all our brave Englishmen.
With the glittering broadsword in amongst them we flew;
They soon tacked about, and away they did go.

Then the Spaniards came out from the town of Sargoon,
With their hands full of bread and their mugs full of rum;
They were so overjoyed, no tongue could express,
Crying: "Down with the French, to the English success!"

Lord Paget came to us and this he did say:
"I thank you bold Fifteenth for your valour this day.
Come, dismount your horses and feed every one,
That we may be ready to fight them again."

214 Robin Hood and the Three Squires

Words and music: traditional Staffordshire, collated, abridged
and arranged by Michael Raven

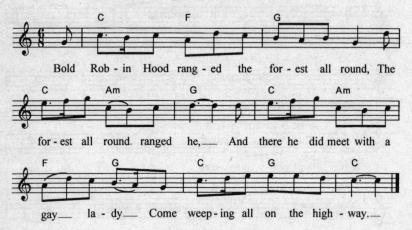

Bold Robin Hood ranged the forest all round,
The forest all round ranged he,
And there he did meet with a gay lady
Come weeping all on the highway.

"Oh why do you weep, my gay lady,
I pray thee come tell unto me?"
"Why I do weep for my three sons
For they are all condemned to die"

"And what have they done", said Jolly Robin;
I pray thee come tell unto me?"
"They've killed sixteen of the King's fallow deer,
And they are all condemned to die."

Then bold Robin went to fair Nottingham town,
To Nottingham town went he;
And there he did meet with an old beggar man
Come weeping all on the highway.

"Then pull off your coat", said Jolly Robin,
"And I will give to you mine;
And fifty bright guineas I shall give you
Beside brandy, good ale, and wine."

Then bold Robin Hood went to fair Nottingham
To Nottingham town went he;
And there he did meet with the master sheriff,
Likewise the squires all three.

"One boon, one boon,"says Jolly Robin,
"One boon, I beg on my knee.
That is for the three squires' sakes
Their hangman I might be."

"Soon granted, soon granted," says the master sheriff
Soon granted unto thee;
And you shall have their gay clothing
And all their white money."

"I'll have none of their gay clothing
Nor none of their white money;
But I'd have three blasts of my bugle-horn
As their souls into heaven may flee."

Then Robin Hood mounted the gallows so high;
He blew both loud and shrill;
One hundred and ten of bold Robin Hood's men
Came tripping all down the green hill.

"Whose men are all these?" said the master sheriff,
"I pray thee come tell unto me."
"Why they are all mine and none of them thine;
They are come for the squires all three."

"Go take them, go take them,"says the master sheriff,;
"Go take them along with thee;
There's never a man in fair Nottingham
 Can do the like of thee."

Braes of Yarrow

Words: traditional, anglicized and adapted by Michael Raven;
music: traditional, fitted by Michael Raven

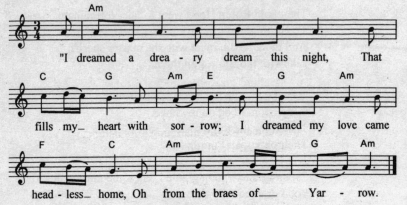

"I dreamed a dreary dream this night,
That fills my heart with sorrow;
I dreamed my love came headless home,
Oh from the Braes of Yarrow.

"Oh true-love mine stay still and dine;
As you have done before-o;"
"Oh I'll be home by hours nine,
And from the Braes of Yarrow."

"Oh are you going to hawk" she says,
"As you have done before-o?
Or are you going to wield your sword,
Upon the Braes of Yarrow?"

"Oh I am not going to hawk" he says,
"As I have done before-o,
But for to meet your brother John,
Upon the Braes of Yarrow."

As he went down the dowy den,
Sorrow went him before-o;
Nine well-wight men lay waiting him,
Upon the Braes of Yarrow.

"I have your sister to my wife,
You think me an unmeet marrow;
But yet one foot will I never flee,
Now from the Braes of Yarrow."

Then four he killed and five did wound,
And laid them to the ground-o;
And he had well nigh won the day
Upon the Braes of Yarrow.

But a cowardly man came him behind,
Our Lady lend him sorrow!
And with a rapier, pierced his heart,
And laid him low on Yarrow.

Now Douglas to his sister's gone,
With much grief and sorrow:
"Go to your love," sister he says,
"He's sleeping sound on Yarrow."

As she went down the dowy den,
Sorrow went her before-o;
She saw her true-love lying slain
Upon the Braes of Yarrow.

She kissed his mouth, she combed his hair,
As she had done before-o;
She wiped the blood that trickled down
Upon the Braes of Yarrow.

Her hair it was three-quarters long,
It hung both sides, and yellow;
She tied it round her white neck bone,
And took her life on Yarrow.

Death and the Lady

Words: traditional; music: traditional, fitted and
adapted by Michael Raven

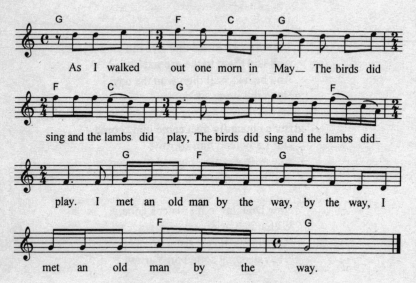

As I walked out one morn in May— The birds did
sing and the lambs did play, The birds did sing and the lambs did—
play. I met an old man by the way, by the way, I
met an old man by the way.

His head was bald, his beard was grey;
His coat was of a myrtle shade.
I asked him what strange counter-ee,
Of what strange place belonged, belonged,
Of what strange place belonged.

"My name is death, cannot you see?
Lords, dukes and ladies bow to me,
And you are one of those branches three,
And you must come with me, with me,
Oh you must come with me."

"I'll give you gold and jewels rare;
I'll give you costly robes to wear;
I'll give you all my wealth in store
To live a few years more, years more,
To live a few years more."

"Fair lady lay your robes aside.
No longer glory in your pride;
And now sweet maid, make no delay
For you must come away, away,
For you must come away."

And not long after this fair maid died;
"Write on my tomb," the lady cried:
" Here lies a poor distressed maid,
Whom death lately betrayed, betrayed,
Whom death lately betrayed."

William Booth

Words: Jon Raven; music: Michael Raven.
William Booth, highwayman, forger and murderer was , indeed, twice
tried, twice hung (in 1812), and twice buried

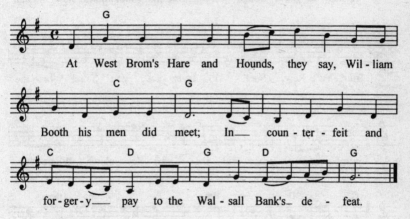

At West Brom's Hare and Hounds, they say, Wil-liam
Booth his men did meet; In— coun-ter-feit and
for-ger-y— pay to the Wal-sall Bank's— de - feat.

His brother's life and a pedlar's too, some swore he took away;
Then tried he was for murder new, but the evidence held no sway.

Dragoons full seven and specials ten rode to the Hare and Hounds,
Where Booth with forgeries was ta'en and carried from the grounds.

At Stafford court he was arraigned and there condemned on high:
The noose around his neck was ranged, but Booth refused to die.

Revived and hung just two hours gone, Booth to his grave was
    ta'en;
Oh there to lie but for a while, till the boundary line was changed.

This verse can also be used as a chorus
Twice tried, twice hung, twice bur-i-ed was Booth of Perry Bar;
Twice tried, twice hung, twice bur-i-ed was Booth of Perry Bar.

Moorlough Shore

Words: traditional Irish; music: traditional, adapted by Michael Raven

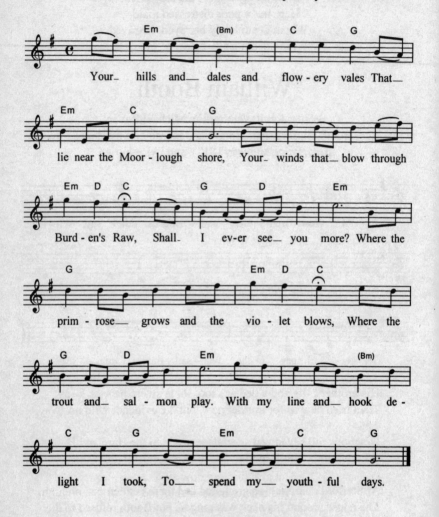

Your hills and dales and flowery vales
That lie near the Moorlough Shore,
Your winds that blow through Burden's Raw,
Shall I ever see you more?
Where the primrose grows and the violet blows,
Where the trout and salmon play.
With my line and hook delight I took,
To spend my youthful days.

As I walked out to meet my girl,
To hear what she would say,
To see if she would take pity on me
Before I would go away.
She said: "I loved an Irish lad,
And he was my only joy,
And ever since I saw his face,
I've loved my soldier boy."

"Maybe your soldier boy was lost
Whilst crossing the raging main,
Or perhaps he's gone with some other girl;
You might never see him again."
"Well, if my soldier boy is lost
He's the one that I adore,
And for seven long years I'll wait for him,
On the banks of the Moorlough Shore."

Farewell to Saint Clare's castle grand;
Farewell to Foggy Hill,
Where the linen waves like bleached silk
And the purling stream runs still.
Near there I spent my youthful days,
But alas they are now all o'er,
And cruelty has banished me
Far away from the Moorlough Shore.

Freedom and Reform

Words: traditional; music: traditional, fitted by Michael Raven

You work-ing men of En - ger - land, who live by dail - ly toil,__ Speak for your rights, bold Eng - lish - men, And__ all through Bri - tain's Isle.__ The ti - tled Tor - ies keep you down Which you can - not en - dure.__ They pass the poor_man with a frown, And the Tor-ies keep you poor.

You working men of England,
Who live by daily toil,
Speak for your rights, bold Englishmen,
And all through Britain's Isle.
The titled Tories keep you down
Which you cannot endure.
They pass the poor man with a frown,
And the Tories keep you poor.

We want no Tory Government,
The poor man to oppress;
They never try to do you good;
The truth you will confess.
The Liberals are the poor man's friend;
To forward all they try.
They'll beat their foes you may depend,
And never will say die.

Then vote for manhood sufferage,
And the ballot too likewise,
For freedom of opinion,
And Englishman doth prize;
And why should not the working man,
Have power to give his vote,
To one that is the poor man's friend,
Through he wears a fustian coat.

Why working men are not to vote,
I cannot understand.
I'd like to know who the taxes pay,
To lords who rule this land.
It's time our laws they altered were,
You'll say it is a bore,
That dual votes should be for rich,
And not one for the poor.

An Englishman is not a slave,
For that was never meant;
Then give the working man his rights;
You'll find he is content.
Give us the Ballot and franchise;
It's the only boon we ask;
Then shouts will rend the skies,
For that will end our task.

Sheath and Knife

Words: traditional, collated and adapted by Michael Raven;
music: traditional arranged by Michael Raven

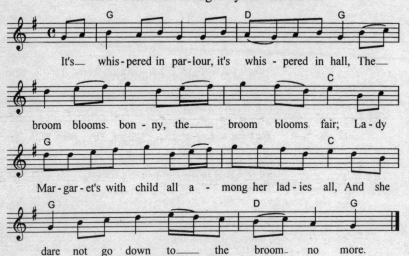

It's— whis-pered in par-lour, it's whis-pered in hall, The— broom blooms. bon-ny, the— broom blooms fair; La-dy Mar-gar-et's with child all a-mong her lad-ies all, And she dare not go down to— the broom— no more.

It's whispered in parlour, it's whispered in hall,
Lady Margaret's with child all among her ladies all.

One lady whispered unto another,
Lady Margaret's with child to Sir Richard her brother.

He's taken his sister down to her father's park,
With his yew-tree bow and arrows there slung to his back.

Now when that you hear me give a loud cry,
Shoot from thy bow and arrow and there let me lie.

He has made a grave that was long and was deep,
And he buried his sister, with the babe all at her feet.

And when he came to his father's court hall,
There was music and minstrels and dancing and all.

O Willie, O Willie, what makes thee in pain?
I have lost a sheath and knife that I'll never see again.

There are ships of my father sailing on the sea,
But such a sheath and knife they can never bring me.

The Welshman

Words: traditional; music: Welsh traditional, adapted and
fitted by Michael Raven

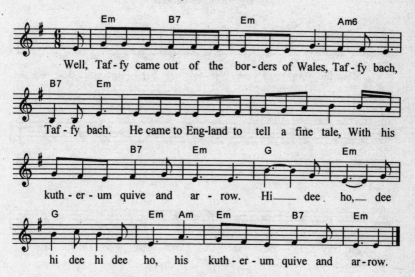

Well, Taf-fy came out of the bor-ders of Wales, Taf-fy bach,
Taf-fy bach. He came to Eng-land to tell a fine tale, With his
kuth-er-um quive and ar-row. Hi___ dee. ho,___ dee
hi dee hi dee ho, his kuth-er-um quive and ar-row.

Taffy went out on a moon shiny night,
He stole a grey mare and swore it was white.

Taffy got up for to ride away,
He was overtaken before it was day.

Taffy was sent to Nottingham jail,
And how to get out could no ways prevail.

Taffy was tried before the Lord Judge,
Sure they won't hang him for such an old drudge.

Taffy he was then condemned for to die,
Which pricked his conscience and made him to cry.

Taffy he mounted the gallows so high,
With all his acquaintances standing by.

Pray give my love to my mother and father,
And likewise my duty to sister and brother.

Pray give my love to the rest of my kin,
And tell them I'm going to heaven in a sling.

Rose of Cashmere

Words: Birmingham broadside; music: traditional, fitted
by Michael Raven

By the flowers of the val-ley all bend-ing with dew, By the

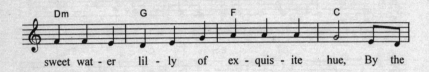

sweet wat-er lil-ly of ex-quis-ite hue, By the

bright sky a-bove us all cloud-less and clear, I___

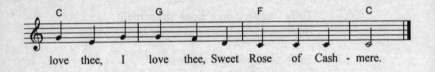

love thee, I love thee, Sweet Rose of Cash-mere.

By the flowers of the valley all bending with dew,
By the sweet water lily of exquisite hue,
By the bright sky above us all cloudless and clear,
I love thee, I love thee, Sweet Rose of Cashmere.

Young Bella of Paradise, shadow of light,
Sweet angel of brighter skies blest being bright,
Oh rest thee or roam thou wilt ever be dear,
For I love thee, I love thee, Sweet Rose of Cashmere.

By that glossy black hair and thy bright beaming eye,
By the bloom on thy cheeks which the roses outvie;
By thy footsteps of lightness that mocks the wild deer,
I love thee, I love thee, Sweet Rose of Cashmere.

Broken-down Gentleman

Words and music English traditional, arranged by Michael Raven

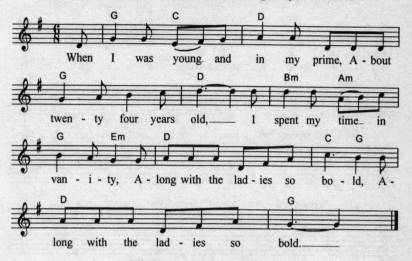

When I was young and in my prime, About twenty four years old, I spent my time in vanity, Along with the ladies so bold, Along with the ladies so bold.

I hired a coach and six bay horses
And servants to wait on me,
For I did intend my money to spend,
And that you can plainly see.

With my silver buckles all round my wrists,
And a cane all in my hand,
All over the nation I did go like,
A farmer's son so grand.

I steered my coach to Epsom races
All on one Derby Day,
And there I did spend ten thousand pounds,
All in the delight of one day,

I steered my coach back home again;
The crops they did run small,
For I was a broken-down gentleman,
And that was the worst of all.

*This song is
also known as
Off to Epsom
Races*

The landlord came all for his rent,
And bailiffs he brought three;
They took away all I had got
And they swore they would have me.

My wife at home she does lament,
And the children around her cry,
While I all in some prison do lie,
Until the day I die.

Waiting for Wages

Words: Jill McLean; music: traditional, fitted by Chris Mordey

It's on a Sat-ur-day af-ter dark, When the pot-ters' wives be-gin to hark, And lis-ten for the men-folks walk And wait there for— their wa-ges. I won-der what the mas-ters think As they buy their lad-ies pearls and mink, And force our men to the pubs to drink, And wait there for— their wa-ges.

In groups of three and four they go
To change their note, but well they
   know,
That ere the evening is through
They'll have spent half of their
   wages.
For he waits until they've eaten
   their fill,
And drunk the ale and paid the bill,
For unless the Landlord's filled
   his till
They'll stay waiting for their
   wages.

Sometimes the master's greed
   is found,
He cuts his wage bill to
   the ground
By giving worthless trinkets
   round,
Instead of paying wages.
And so the family starves again
Though they work so hard again;
It's a hopeless job to feed all
   them
Upon starvation wages.

I Would the Wars were Over

Words: traditional; music: Michael Raven, incorporating
a traditional fragment

In the mea-dow one morn-ing when pear-ly with_ dew A__ fair pret-ty mai-den plucked vi-o-lets_ blue. I heard her clear voice mak-ing all the woods ring: "Oh my love is in Flan-ders to fight for the king, And I would that the wars were all o-ver, Oh I would that the wars_ were all done.

27.7.1999

"I'll pluck the red robin so jaunty and gay;
Yet I have my Robin, but he's far away.
His jacket is red - and cheeks - as the rose;
He sings of his Nell as to battle he goes.
And I would that the wars were all over,
Oh I would that the wars were all done.

"Ten thousand of bluebells now welcome the spring;
Oh when will the church bells for victory ring?
And the soldiers return and all England rejoice?
Oh then I'll be wed to the lad of my choice.
And I would that the wars were all over,
Oh I would that the wars were all done."

Widow Woman's Daughter

Words and music: traditional, arranged Michael Raven

Oh there was a wid-ow wo-man from the West Moor-lands And she nev-er had a daught-er but the one; And her on-ly ad-vice was by day or by night To nev-er give her mai-den-head to one. "Hold your tongue, dear moth-er," says she And there-fore do not let it be For there was a jol-ly sol-dier in the Queen's Life-Guards; Last night he stole my maid-en-head from me."

Oh there was a widow woman from the West Moorlands
And she never had a daughter but the one;
And her only advice was by night or by day
To never give her maidenhead to one.
"Hold your tongue, dear mother," says she
"And therefore do not let it be
For there was a jolly soldier in the Queen's Life Guards
Last night he stole my maidenhead from me."

"Oh go, oh go, you saucy jade
And therefore do not let it be,
And bring me back the maidenhead you lost last night,
Or another night you'll never stay with me."
Now she's to the soldier gone,
Her heart both light and free,
Saying: "Give me back the maidenhead you stole last night
For me mammy she's angry with me."

He catched her by the middle so small,
And he threw her on to the bed,
And he turned up her heels where her head ought to be
And he's give her back her maidenhead.
Now she's to her mammy gone,
Her heart both light and free,
Saying: "I'm as clear of all mankind
Since the first night you had me."

That fared well and so passed by,
Till the soldier's wedding it came on;
And the widow woman dressed up her daughter so grand
With a rose in every hand.
"Who is that," cried the bride's daddy,
"That stands so fine and fair?"
"It's the widow woman's daughter from the West Moorlands
And she tells her mammy all."

"Oh how can she do it, oh how can she do it,
How can she do it for shame?
For these nine long nights I have lain with my love,
And I'm sure I never told anyone."
"Well, if it's nine long nights you've lain with your love,
Another night you'll never lie with me,"
And he took the widow's daughter from the West Moorlands

Irish Girl

Words and music: traditional, arranged Michael Raven

As I walked out one May morning down by a riverside,
In gazing all around me an Irish girl I spied.
So red and rosy were her cheeks and coal black was her hair,
And costly were the robes of gold this Irish girl did wear.

Her shoes were made of Spanish leather, all sprinkled o'er with dew.
She wrung her hands, she tore her hair, crying: "Oh what shall I do?
I'm going home, I'm going home, I'm going home," said she.
"How shall I go a-roving and slight my own Johnny?"

I wish I was a butterfly, I'd fly to my love's breast,
And if I were a linnet I would sing my love to rest.
And if I was a nightingale I would sing till the morning clear.
I'd sit and sing for you, Johnny, For I once loved you so dear.

I wish I was a red rosebud that in the garden grew,
And if I was that gardener to my love I would prove true,
There is not one month throughout the year when my love
    I wouldn't renew;
With flowers three I'd garland thee, sweet William,
    thyme and rue.

I wish I was in Dublin town a-sitting on the grass,
With a bottle of whiskey in my hand and on my knee a lass.
I'd call for liquor merrily, I'd spend my money free,
With a rant and a roar all along the shore, let the winds
    blow high or low.

Betsy Bell and Mary Gray

Words: traditional; music:
traditional Flemish, fitted by Michael Raven

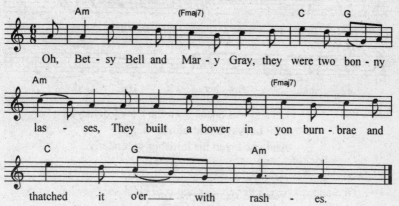

They thatched it o'er with rushes green;
They thatched it o'er with heather,
But the plague came from the burrows town,
And slew them both together.

They thought to lie in Methven church,
Among their noble kin,
But they must lie in Stronach high,
To make amends their sin.

Lass from the Low Country

Words and music: traditional, arranged Michael Raven

Oh she was a lass from the Low Coun-try, And he was a lord of high de - gree, And she loved his lord - ship so ten-der-ly, Oh sor-ow; sing sor - row, Now she sleeps in the val - ley Where the wild flow - ers nod, And no - bo - dy knows she loved him, But her - self and God.

Oh she was a lass from the Low Country,
And he was a lord of high degree,
And she loved his lordship so tenderly.

Oh sorrow, sing sorrow;
Now she sleeps in the valley
Where the wild flowers nod,
And nobody knows she loved him,
But herself and God.

One morn when the sun was on the mead,
He passed her by on his milk-white steed.
She smiled and she spoke but he paid no heed.

If you be a lass from the Low Country,
Don't love no lord of high degree,
For they've got no heart and no sympathy.

Rose in June

Words and music: traditional, from Dave Jones, arranged Michael Raven

The rose in June's not half so sweet As kis-ses when true lov-ers meet. So let it be ear-ly, late or soon I will en-joy my rose in June. Rose in June, rose in June, I will en-joy my rose in June.

The rose in June's not half so sweet
As kisses when two lovers meet.

So let it be early, late or soon
I will enjoy my rose in June.
Rose in June, rose in June,
I will enjoy my rose in June.

The shepherd leads his flocks to the fold,
Let the weather be wet or cold.

Dave Jones
founded the
Bromyard
Folk Festival
and revived
many folk
customs in the
Putley area of
Herefordshire

Then I'll cut down the myrtle tree,
To make a fine bower for Sally and me.

Sweet Betsey she carries the sweet milking pail,
Sweet Betsy she rests at every stile.

The violets make the meadows so gay,
None with my roses can array.

Primroses make the valley so neat,
None with my roses can compete.

Bonny Light Horseman

Words: traditional; music: Michael Raven

When Bon-ney com-man-ded his ar-mies to stand, He le-velled his can-nons right o-ver the land; He— le-velled his can-nons his— vic-t'ry— to— gain, And my bon-ny light horse-man in the wars he was slain. Bro-ken- heart-ed I wan-der, bro-ken-heart-ed— I'll re-main, Since my bon-ny light horse-man in the wars he was slain.

If I was a small bird and had wings to fly,
I would fly o'er the salt sea where my love does lie;
And with my fond wings I'd beat o'er his grave,
And kiss the pale lips that lie cold in the clay.

The dove she laments for her mate as she flies:
"Oh where, tell me where, is my darling?" she cries;
And where in the world is there one to compare
To my bonny light horseman who was slain in the war.

I shall dress in men's clothing, to the regiment I'll go;
I'll be a true subject and fight all our foes.
I would count it an honour if I could obtain
To die in the field where my darling was slain.

Review in **Folk Roots** of Michael Raven and Joan Mills' *Songs and Solos* MRCD68

Get past the forbidding cover shot and you will find something quite exceptional. Raven is a guitarist of unquestionable but carefully controlled virtuosity and Mills has the heretical idea that you can successfully sing folksongs in your own, everyday unaffected voice.

Pretty well everything here is either traditional or of Raven's making. He's arranged it all including a couple of A. E. Housman poems, and not put a foot wrong as far as I'm concerned. The instrumentals use a lot of technique and harmonic development more commonly found on the flamenco and classical guitar than in the folk arena but what comes through, rather than any flashiness, is his sheer command of the instrument and his material.

Joan Mills sings in an immediately attractive voice and sparing use of decoration, sensitively accompanied by Raven's guitar. Her unforced, natural approach is absolutely fine by me, especially on Irish Girl and Widow Woman's Daughter. She does just enough to put the songs across, not imposing herself any further than that. This economy of approach extends to the avoidance of editing and multi-tracking - they seem to cope perfectly well without. *Nick Beale*

Review in **Folk North-West** of Michael Raven and Joan Mills' *Songs and Solos* MRCD68

Mike Raven has been researching and writing books about folk music, writing tunes for guitar and generally immersing himself in 'the music' for many, many years. He is, as a result, a well-respected authority on a wide range of musical styles. For some time this work has restricted his opportunities to perform on the folk club circuit, so, it was with some delight that I recently received this CD featuring Mike and his singing partner, Joan.

The performances here are quite idiosyncratic but nevertheless classic in every respect. Mike's guitar work is stunning in its intricacy, combining classical and folk styles in a fusion of complex tunes, many of which are self-penned. Joan's superb voice is clear and crystal-like reflecting her Irish connections and is matched superbly by Mike's meticulous arrangements.

There is no hype or recording trickery here and the result is as near a perfect reproduction of a live performance as it is possible to achieve. This is music that demands your attention and rightly deserves it. *Derek Gifford*

MICHAEL RAVEN CATALOGUE

If you experience any difficulty in obtaining these books and recordings from your local music shop they can be supplied to you post free direct from the publisher:

Michael Raven,
Yew Tree Cottage,
Jug Bank, Ashley,
Market Drayton,
Shropshire,
TF9 4NJ
Tel: 01630 672304

Note: all cassettes cost £6.50.

GUITAR MUSIC

The Complete Guitarist
Michael Raven
Price £12.95
Universally acclaimed by the trade press as "the finest classical guitar tutor available today." Follows the Associated Board syllabus. Introductions to folk-blues and flamenco. Assumes no prior knowledge. Classical and modern harmony and special techniques explained in great detail. Includes 64 complete solos which range from lute music to classical studies and arrangements of popular songs. "Unreservedly recommended," Charles Scott, *Classical Guitar*. 9th edition, 172 pages, A4 size.

The Guitarist's Good Book
Michael Raven
Price £7.50
Easy arrangements of 82 well known songs, traditional tunes and hymns. Complete with words and chord symbols for those who wish to strum simple accompaniments. Widely used by absolute beginners. Staff notation only. The solo guitar arrangements provide useful alternative study material. "Detailed instructions, excellent arrangements, tremendous value for money ...unreservedly recommended." *Fretwire* A4 size, 96 pages.

Popular Songs for Guitar 1
Michael Raven
Price £4.50
First published in 1976 and still going strong. Easy but musically satisfying arrangements of 15 timeless tunes: Danny Boy, Minuetto Allegretto, Now the Carnival is Over, Plaisir d'Amour, Morning has Broken, Return to Sorento, Those were the Days, Scarborough Fair, Amazing Grace, Guantanamera, Midnight in Moscow, etc. All the music is printed in both staff notation and tablature. 32 pages, A4 size. **Companion Cassette:** all the music in book 1 is on Side One of the cassette. On Side Two is all the music in Popular Songs for Guitar book 2. Total playing time 46 minutes.

Popular Songs for Guitar 2
Michael Raven
Price £4.50
Another 17 well known tunes amongst which are two of the Rodrigo Guitar Concerto themes and a performance arrangement of The Entertainer. Other tunes include El Condor Pasa, The Sloop John B, Waltzing Matilda and Viva Espana. All the music is in both staff notation and tablature. 32 pages. A4 size. **Companion Cassette:** all the music of book 2 is on Side Two of the cassette. On Side One is all the music in Book 1. Total playing time 46 minutes. Out of print in 1999.

Popular Tunes for Guitar 1
Michael Raven
Price £4.50
Easy but musically satisfying solo guitar arrangements of eight popular tunes - The Green Leaves of Summer (from the film The Alamo), With God on our Side (Bob Dylan), Portsmouth (Mike Oldfield), Wooden Heart (Elvis Presley), etc. All the music is in both staff notation and tablature. Also included is the popular concert solo by Michael Raven, A Welsh Fantasy. 32 pages, A4 size. **Companion Cassette:** all the music in this book is on Side One of the cassette together with recordings of Eight Traditional Tunes in Tablature. On Side

Two is the music to Book 2. Playing time 60 minutes.

Popular Tunes for Guitar 2
Michael Raven
Price £4.50
A selection of 16 well known tunes in easy solo guitar arrangements. Titles include: Never on a Sunday, theme from the Onedin Line, Masters of War, Lord of the Dance, It's a Long Way to Tipperary, House of the Rising Sun, Limelight etc. Printed here too is Choro y Danza, a full scale concert guitar solo by Michael Raven. All the music is in both staff notation and tabulature. 32 pages, A4 size. **Companion Cassette:** all the music in this book is recorded on Side Two of the cassette. On Side One is the music to Book 1.

Eight Traditional Tunes in Tablature
Michael Raven
Price £1.50
These arrangements of 8 attractive little tunes make few technical demands. 8 pages, A4 size. **Companion Cassette:** these tunes are recorded at the end of Side One on the Popular Tunes for Guitar Books 1 and 2 cassette.

A Variety of Guitar Music 1
Michael Raven
Price £7.50
67 pieces: 16th and 17th Century dances; Classical and Romantic music; folk tunes; flamenco solos and ragtime and blues. This book has been in print since 1968 and was the first collection that we published. All the music is in tablature, and most is also in staff notation. "It has a rhyme and reason all its own." *Stephan Grossman*. 80 pages A4 size.
Recording: some of the music is played by Michael Raven on the CD, *Retrospective.*

A Variety of Guitar Music 1 (Revised)
Michael Raven
Price £7.50
A selection of pieces from the original best-selling book, redrawn and printed in both staff notation and tablature, except for the long flamenco Soleares which is in tablature only. 64 pages, A4 size.
Recording: Much of the music has been recorded on the *Retrospective* CD

and on other albums.

A Variety of Guitar Music 2
Michael Raven
Price £5.00
Music in a variety of styles: Buckdancer's Choice, El Paso Waltz, Ragtime Annie, Wilson's Wild, Coventry Carol, March of Brian Boru, Alegrias (a full length flamenco guitar solo) etc. Most pieces are only of moderate difficulty. All the music is printed in staff notation and tablature. 40 pages, A4 size. **Companion Cassette:** all the music, note for note as printed, is recorded on Side One of the cassette. On Side Two is all the music printed in The Chant of Falsity (see below). Playing time 70 minutes.

A Variety of Guitar Music 3
Michael Raven
Price £7.50
30 solos in a variety of styles including a set of original compositions by Michael Raven and an "off the record" transcription of the magnificent Tarantos, a show-stopping flamenco guitar solo of 5 minutes' duration, first recorded by Michael Raven on the LP A Miscellany of Guitar Music. All the music is in both tablature and staff notation. 64 pages A4 size. **Companion Cassette:** all the music, note for note as printed. Duration approximately 50 minutes. Out of print in 1999.

The Chant of Falsity
Michael Raven
Price £4.50
25 pieces in many different styles. This is really another Variety of Guitar Music. The titles include Rhumba Habanera, Moorish Zambra, a set of four colourful Sevillanas dances from Spain, Rag in C major, Sage Leaf, Give me your Hand (a lovely Irish aire), Mozart Quadrille, Villanella etc.
All the music is printed in both staff notation and tablature. 32 pages, A4 size. **Companion Cassette:** all the music in this book is recorded on Side Two of the cassette; on Side One is recorded the contents of A Variety of Guitar Music Book 2. Total playing time 70 minutes.

English Folk Guitar 1
Michael Raven
Price £7.50
Devoted almost entirely to song
accompaniment with off-the-record
transcriptions of pieces by Nic Jones and
arrangements in the style of Martin
Carthy and many others. Words to all
the songs; melody lines in staff notation;
guitar part in tablature; details of 10
different tunings; tablature thoroughly
explained; 29 songs each with an
analytical commentary. The first and
still the only book devoted to the subject.
72 page, A4 size.
Recordings: there is not a companion
cassette but Death and the Lady, The
Jolly Highwayman, The Captain's
Apprentice and Ladies Don't go a-
Thievin' are available on The Folk
Heritage Recordings, a compilation of
two LPs recorded by Michael Raven and
Joan Mills. Playing time 60 minutes.
Out of print in 1999.

English Folk Guitar 2
Michael Raven
Price £7.50
This book is devoted to solo instrumental
playing and in particular to styles
developed from medieval lute and harp
traditions. There are 37 tunes - the
Cobbler, Cushion Dance, Adson's
Sarabande, Drums of Johore, Maid of
Provence, Glendower's Jig, Dove's
Figary, Hills of Glenorchy, Road to
Lisdoonvarna, etc. All the music is
printed in tablature and staff notation.
Most are not at all difficult and being
such good and timeless tunes are
rewarding to work on. 64 pages A4 size.
Companion Cassette: has a playing
time of 58 minutes.

English Folk Guitar 3
Michael Raven
Price £7.50
Like book 2 this is devoted entirely to
solo instrumental pieces, 31 in all.
Included are the concert solos: Black is
the Colour and The Miller's Song by
Michael Raven, The Little Heathy Hill
by Nic Jones, The Siege of Delhi by
Martin Carthy, and a good selection of
jigs, reels, aires and morris dance tunes.
All the music is in tablature and staff
notation. 64 pages, A4 size. **Companion**
cassette: all the music exactly as printed
in the book except the Siege of Delhi and
the Little Heathy Hill. Playing time 56
minutes.

English Folk Guitar 4
Michael Raven
Price £7.50
Transcriptions of all the guitar solos,
songs and accompaniments on the CD
Recital. Titles include: Lass from the
Low Country, Ruth Ellis, Fortune My
Foe, Dancing Delilah, Raglan Road,
Biker's Song, Welsh tunes and English
traditional songs. 28 pieces in all. Most
of the music is in both staff notation and
tablature. 64 pages, 9 x 12 inches.
Companion CD: 80 minutes duration.

Popular Music for Guitar
Michael Raven
Price £7.50
Contains a selection of 36 well known
tunes in easy to moderately difficult
arrangements - the Eton Boating Song,
Schubert's Serenade, Cwm Rhondda, Fur
Elise, Bluebell Polka, Crimond, Claire de
Lune, O Sole Mio, As I Went to
Walsingham, Daisy Bell etc. The
foreword suggests ways of using short
tunes to make extended pieces. All the
music is printed in both staff notation and
tablature. 64 pages, A4 size. **Companion**
Cassette: contains performances of all
the music in the book. Playing time
54 minutes.

Popular Classics for Guitar
Michael Raven
Price £7.50
Carefully selected to be within the range
of the average player the contents are: 24
studies by Carcassi; three gavottes by
J.S. Bach, three renaissance lute pieces
(all recorded by Julian Bream); Suite in
D and Suite in E by Michael Raven;
Maria Eleanor; English aires and dances
and studies by Sor, Guilliani and Carulli.
All the music is in staff notation and
about half is also in tablature. 64 pages,
A4 size. **Recording:** there is not a
companion cassette but some of the
music has been recorded by Michael
Raven on the LP (and cassette)
A Miscellany of Guitar Music which
is still available.

Easy Duets for Guitar
Joseph Kuffner
Price £4.50
In his day Joseph Kuffner (1776-1856) was the most celebrated composer in Europe, eclipsing even his illustrious friend Beethoven. These easy duets are very easy indeed, yet musically most rewarding. What is more the top line stands complete as a solo composition. Printed here are Opus 80 and Opus 87 complete with a biography of Kuffner. These 37 duets are the best of their kind. There is no Companion cassette.
32 pages, A4.

Michael Raven:
Guitar Music 1 and 2
Michael Raven
Price £10.00
Books 1 and 2 in one volume. 76 pieces which include a grand concert solo arrangement of Bobby Shaftoe in gipsy style; arrangements of traditional tunes such as Little Birds of the Mountain, Slaughter House and the English Echo; and new pieces such as Kellman's Harp, the Ratchup Pipes and Rag in G major. All in staff notation and tablature. 128 pages, 9 inches x 12 inches. **Companion Cassettes:** all the music, note for note as written, has been recorded on two 60 minute cassettes, one for each book, They can be ordered separately.

Music for Guitar
Michael Raven
Price £12.00
"A Magnum Opus." Charles Scott *Classical Guitar.* 155 easy to moderately difficult arrangements of a variety of music: lute pieces, popular songs, flamenco, folk tunes, country dances, original compositions etc. and some full concert solos. Titles include: Clun Castle Dirge, Carminda's Aire, Slain in Egypt, Colombiana, Pradoe Pavan, Black Queen, Jota, Tanguillio, Earl's Entry, Dead of Rajistan, Stockport Carnival Dance, etc. Note: this is not a compilation of previously published music. 256 pages, 9 x 12 inches, sewn in sections. **Companion Cassettes:** five cassettes, £4.00 each. The recordings were made using my old Ramirez flamenco guitar and a synthesised guitar.

Michael Raven:
Guitar Music 3 and 4
Michael Raven
Price £10.00
Books 3 and 4 in one volume. 68 pieces which include Gipsy Part Two, a performance piece incorporating folk tunes and flamenco; English traditional dances, Irish polkas, new music and arrangements of popular songs such as Ain't She Sweet, Mendeissohn's Wedding March and a full notation of the Lichfield Bower Greenhill Processional, Mike Raven's best known concert solo. All in staff notation and tablature. 128 pages, 9 inches x 12 inches. **Companion Cassettes:** all the music note for note as written has been recorded on two 60 minute cassettes, one for each book. They can be ordered separately.

An English Collection 1
Michael Raven
Price £2.50
11 pieces for solo guitar. Titles include: Off to California, Jigg Ashling, Beatrice Hill's Reel, Dowland's Alman etc. Easy to moderate; staff notation and tablature; 16 pages, A4.

Silent Field
Michael Raven
Price £7.50
36 pieces for solo guitar. Titles include: Mandrake, Mexican Serenade, Mills of Strata Marcella, Roaring Hornpipe, Jockey to the Fair, Mulberry Garden etc. and there are 14 Playford dances, 6 new pieces, 3 Scottish dances, 2 Flemish Maying songs and the famous Autumn Leaves. Easy to moderate; Staff notation and tablature, 64 pages; 9 x 12 inches. **Companion Cassette:** 63 minutes duration.

Star of Belle Isle
Michael Raven
Price £7.50
44 titles for solo guitar. Contents include: Four Short Pieces; Popular Songs (Don't Bring Lulu, Sicilian Waltz, etc.); Celtic Tunes: Flowers of the Forest, Wicklow Hornpipe, She Moves Through the Fair, etc; 17thC and 18thC Dances; and 16 English Country Dances (Abbot's Bromley Horn Dance etc.) Easy to moderate; staff notation and tablature;

64 pages, 9 x 12 inches. **Companion Cassette:** 69 minutes playing time.

Soulton Hall
Michael Raven
Price £7.50
36 aires, dances and cafe songs for solo guitar by Michael Raven from English country dances to Latin American pieces. Titles include: Cafe Song in E minor, Wolf's Head Polka, Christmas at Soulton Hall, Severn Boating Song, Watling Street Rag, Cajun Exile, Cadfael's Chant etc. Staff notation and tablature; 64 pages, 9 x l2 inches. **Companion Cassette:** Duration 60 minutes.

Delbury Dervish
Michael Raven
Price £7.50
36 pieces for solo guitar comprising: 14 hymns (Richmond, Zachary, Eternal Father, Gonfalon Royal, etc.); 9 Thomas Hardy fiddle tunes arranged as The Dorchester Suite (Laura, Irish Devil, Speed the Plough, Volage Quadrille, etc.); and 13 Cafe Songs and Country Dances (Bringewood Waters, A49 Reel. Lazy Jane, etc.). Staff notation and tablature; 64 pages, 9 x 12 inches. **Companion Cassette:** 60 minutes duration.

Wizard Beguildy
Michael Raven
Price £7.50
35 English aires and country dances for solo guitar. Titles include: Argeers, Horsehay Two Stick Dance, Rosebud in June, Cat Tails Polka, Nutting Girl, Cherry Garden, Shirlett Forest Reels, Two French Brawls etc. and a curiosity, Freight Train as a flamenco waltz. Staff notation and tablature; 64 pages; 9 x 12 inches. **Companion Cassette:** 59 minutes.

Lucy's Frolic
Michael Raven
Price £7.50
35 aires and dances for solo guitar. Titles include: Badger Two Step, Clun Forest Dirge, Bathsheba's Hymn, Blackbird Fly No More, Lark in the Clear Air, Morrison's Jig, Confess, Lord Anson For Ever, Ode to Lydia etc. and a flamenco Garrotin (transcribed from the Guitar Magic LP). Staff notation and tablature; 64pages; 9 x 12 in. **Companion Cassette:** 55 minutes.

Songs and Solos
Michael Raven
Price £7.50
Transcriptions from the CD of all 24 guitar solos and 6 of the 13 songs (sung by Joan Mills) and their accompaniments. Tunes include: Nottingham Swing, Mainstone Hornpipe, Newcastle (what a good tune that is), Lament for Peter Bellamy and Fred Jordan's Galliard. Amongst the songs are: Flowers in Her Hair, Octopus Dancing, Lament for Owain Glyndwr, Land of Lost Content, Mirror of My Mind and Midnight in the City etc. Staff notation and tablature; 64 pages,9 x 12 inches. **Companion CD:** 80 minutes duration. One guitar (steel strung Lowden) and one voice.

Welsh Guitar
Michael Raven
Price £7.50
Transcriptions from the CD of all 42 Welsh aires, dances and harp pieces arranged for solo guitar. Easy to moderate difficulty. Titles include: Grey Cuckoo, Sailor's Grave, Sweet Richard, Lady Treffael's Conceit, Spanish Minuet, Missing Boat, Watching the Wheat, John Francis, Lark's Elegy, etc. Michael Raven was born in Cardiff and went to school at Towyn. Staff notation and tablature; 64 pages, 9 x 12 inches. **Companion CD:** 70 minutes.

A Shropshire Lad
Michael Raven
Price £7.50
Transcriptions from the CD of all 20 Welsh aires and dances arranged for solo guitar and all 17 Housman poems set to traditional melodies (sung by Joan Mills) complete with guitar accompaniments in staff notation and tablature. Some lovely and unusual music. Solos include: Megan's Daughter, Rhoslan Reel, White Rose of Summer, Clover, Farewell to Llangyfelach and Galaru etc. Most of Housman's best loved verses are here: Bredon Hill, On Wenlock Edge, Midnights of November, Is My Team Ploughing, Shrewsbury Jail etc. Solos

and song accompaniments in staff notation and tablature; 64 pages; 9 x 12 inches. **Companion CD** 80 minutes duration.

FOLK MUSIC

1,000 English Country Dance Tunes
Michael Raven
Price £20.00
Enlarged, revivsed, reset and now nearly 1,200 tunes. The largest single collection of English country dance tunes ever published. Jigs, triple jigs, set dances, waltzes, reels, hornpipes, polkas, quicksteps, Schottisches etc., with special features on Morris. Sword and Ceremonial tunes, the Northumbrian pipes, and facsimile reproductions of the complete first editions of the Beggar's Opera (1729) and The English Dancing Master (1651). Widely acclaimed by professional folk and early music musicians. 336 pages, 12 x 9 inches; laminated cover, sewn in sections

Reynardine
Michael Raven
Price £7.50
This book contains a selection of music from the repertoire of a popular folk band. There are 72 pages of songs and dance tunes all of which are suitable for fiddle, flute, tin whistle, mandolin, bouzouki and guitar. The tunes are arranged in performance sets and many are printed complete with harmony lines and counter melodies. All have suggested harmonies indicated by chord symbols. The vocal music ranges from ancient ballads to industrial protest songs. The instrumental music includes jigs, reels, set dances, hornpipes, mazurkas, slides, polkas, aires and listening tunes, both traditional and newly composed. **Recordings:** some of the music has been recorded on The Reynardine Tapes CD.

Hynde Horn
Michael Raven
Price £7.50
A combined edition of two books: 'Ballads and Songs from Britain', and 'Aires and Dances of Wales'. Songs recorded by June Tabor, Steeleye Span

and others, but also many little known traditional masterpieces and a handful of contemporary songs such as The Great Train Robbery, and Hyrmn to Che Guevara. 68 pages, A4 size.

A Shropshire Lad
A. E. Housman-Michael Raven
Price £3.00
A selection of 18 Housman poems set to some very fine traditional tunes by Michael Raven. Harmonies are suggested by chord symbols but most of these songs sound well unaccompanied. The First Edition is limited to 500 and the books (16 pages A4 size) are numbered and signed by Michael Raven.

Raven's Nest
Michael Raven
Price £4.50
Rural, industrial and contemporary folksongs, some with guitar accompaniment, all with chord symbols; 41 titles including a few poems and riddles: Bold Robin Hood, Stafford Pageant Song, Tim Evans' Dance, Darlaston Dogfight, My Last Farewell to Stirling, Wedgefield Wake, Queen of the Night, Midnight City, Mirror of My Mind, Over the Wall, Brave Collier Lads. etc. 32 pages, A4 size. By using a condensed landscape format this book has almost twice the amount of material normally contained in a volume of this size and price. In short, it is a bargain! **Recordings:** There is not a Companion cassette but most of the songs have been recorded and details are given in the book.

Folksongs of the Low Countries
Michael Raven
Price £4.50
A collection of 20 songs and dance tunes from the Netherlands and Belgium with English translations. Each song tune has also been arranged as a guitar solo. There are some excellent tunes here - Leonore (recorded by Michael Raven on A Miscellany of Guitar Music, is especially attractive), Snow White Bird, Pierlala, and the Maying Song etc. The Belgian group, Rum, has also recorded some of these tunes. 32 pages, A4 size.

Kempion

*Edited by David Oxley
and Michael Raven
Price £4.50*

This book contains a collection of 30 mainly Irish and Scottish songs and dance tunes as played by a professional folk band. These are genuine off-the-record transcriptions of actual performances, largely notated by members of the group themselves. All the music printed here has been tried and tested over many years of playing. The result is a first class collection of jigs, reels, hornpipes polkas and aires, arranged in performance sets and interspersed with songs and ballads. 32 pages, A4 size.

John O'Barbary

*Michael Raven
Price £4.50*

A collection of 32 traditional songs and dance tunes. Some are little known; some are from the repertoires of Silly Wizard, Nic Jones, June Tabor, The Bothy Band etc. Titles include, John O'Barbary, Tasman's Hunt, The Strayaway Child, Young Redin, The Wanton Seed, Jackie Tar, etc. The melody lines are in staff notation with chord symbols and there are some suggested harmonies and guitar accompaniments in tablature.
32 pages, A4 size.

The Jolly Machine

*Michael Raven
Price £4.50*

Sub-titled: 'Songs of Industrial Protest and Social Discontent from the West Midlands'. Contains some excellent but little known songs from the Potteries. Titles include: Waiting for Wages, The Tommy Note, Charlie's Song, The Nailmakers' Strike, The Dudley Boys etc. 32 pages, A4 size. **Companion CD:** Many of the 23 songs have been recorded by Michael Raven and Joan Mills with Derby folk group Saga. See The Halliard : Jon Raven / Jolly Machine, CDMR77.

Victoria's Inferno

*Jon Raven
Price £3.50*

A unique collection of 72 songs of the old mines, mills, manufactures, canals and railways with comprehensive notes, full texts and melody lines with chord symbols. These 18th and 19th Century songs of colliers, cutlers, nailmakers, potters, shipwrights and railmen etc. were mostly written at times of strike, strife or disaster and are as much a social statement as a collection of songs. Jon Raven is a leading authority on industrial folksongs. He is the author of many books on the subject, and has been a consultant on numerous radio and television programmes. 192 pages, paperback size.

Urban and Industrial Songs of the Black Country and Birmingham

*Jon Raven
Price £15.00*

A beautifully produced hardback book finely printed on quality laid paper. This work, an outstanding study in industrial folksong, was supported by grants from the Leverhulme Trust and West Midlands Arts. 129 songs with text that describes their historical and social setting by Jon Raven, indisputably the leading authority in this field. 258 pages, A5 clothbound hardback.

Tarlton's Jests

*Edited by Michael Raven
Price £3.00*

Richard Tarlton (d. 1588) was a humble Shropshire farm labourer who became famous throughout England as Queen Elizabeth I's Court Jester. He was also an actor, a musician and one of the country's finest swordsmen - a Master of Fence. Tarlton's Jests were published shortly after he died and were an instant best-seller, a phenomenon of the age. The modern reader will find much of the humour slight. Nevertheless, the Jests are important as an adjunct to social studies of the time, especially of Shakespeare, who knew Tarlton well. This edition is a facsimile of the book published by the Shakespeare Society in 1844. The original 39 pages have been reproduced on 16 landscape A4 pages.

Ross Workhouse Songbook

*Michael Raven
Price £6.50*

Transcriptions of all the songs, guitar accompaniments, guitar solos, poems and viola tunes on the *Songs and Dances of*

Herefordshire CD which has contributions from Pat and Roy Palmer. Includes lovely versions of Lowlands of Holland, Dives and Lazarus, Milkmaid's Song and Sheffield Park, and some fine dance tunes such as Jack of the Green and Mr. Baskerville's Volt. Music in staff notation only. 48 pages, 9 x 12 inches.

RECORDER, FLUTE AND TIN WHISTLE MUSIC

Popular Songs for Recorder 1
Michael Raven
Price £2.00
These 32 tunes were carefully chosen to have lasting appeal. All around my Hat, Guantanamera, The Entertainer, Lord of the Dance, Wooden Heart, Green Leaves of Summer, Portsmouth, Return to Sorrento, Morning has Broken, Amazing Grace, In an English Country Garden etc. Breathing points are marked and chord symbols are given. This little book is attractive to young people and has been in print since 1977. It has 32 pages, A5 size.

Popular Songs for Recorder 2
Michael Raven
Price £4.00
The music is written a little larger than usual to help young people. Amongst the 46 tunes are: A Policeman's Lot, Because You're Mine, El Condor Pasa, Malaguenia, Mexican Hat Dance, Sloop John B, Viva Espana, Whisky in the Jar, Z Cars, Jamaica Farewell, A Bunch of Thyme, Onedin Line Theme etc. Chord symbols are printed above the melody lines and there is a descant recorder note chart. 32 pages, A4 size.

Popular Tunes for Recorder
Michael Raven
Price £4.00
Also most suitable for the flute and the tin whistle. Indeed, there is a full explanation of how the non-music reader can entabulate staff notation for the tin whistle. The contents include the Dark Island (Band of the Black Watch), March of Brian Boru, (James Galway), Morning Dew, Black Waterside (Led Zeppelin), Sonny Brogan's Mazurca (The Chieftains), Masters of War (Bob Dylan),

Cuckoo's Nest (Albion Dance Band), My Kindly Sweetheart (Silly Wizard) etc. 35 tunes in all, 32 pages, A4 size.

The Tin Whistle Tutor
Michael Raven
Price £3.50
Since it was first published in 1977 this book has established itself as the most thorough tutor for the humble tin whistle ever printed. The player is taught how to read music as well as the tin whistle. There are clear diagrams, note charts, and also instruction on ornamentation and entabulation. Pieces to play include Sheebeg Sheemor, Give Me Your Hand and Aymara Indian Dance. 32 pages, A4 size. Out of print in 1999.

POETRY

Song of the Fox
Michael Raven
Price £2.50
A collection of 83 original songs, ballads and poems by Michael Raven. Titles include: Lines on Gatley Park, Sons of Glyndwr (from which was derived the name of a Welsh nationalist party), Song of the Fox, Why oh Wye? Dark-haired Daughters, Little Sparrow, Down in South Australia, Foxy's Flying, I am a Rabbit, etc. Second Edition with many new poems added. 64 pages, 4.5 x 7 inches paperback.

TOPOGRAPHICAL GUIDES

Staffordshire and the Black Country
Michael Raven
Price £10, paperback; £20 hardback
A 420 page, A5 book with 40 pages of full colour photographs and some 750 black and white photographs. This book is a comprehensive gazetteer describing every town, village and hamlet in the county, their history, geography, customs and special points of interest. "Thoroughly researched and attractively presented." "He has an eye and an ear for the unusual…" This book took over a year to write, full time, and is now accepted to be the most comprehensive guide to the county in print. Superb, a

book I will treasure." Librarian, West
Bromwich.

A Shropshire Gazetteer
Michael Raven
Price £15: a few hardbacks at £25
"It has to be the definitive book on
Shropshire." Shropshire Alternative.
The researching and writing of this book
took nearly two years, full time, seven
days a week. It is a comprehensive
survey of of the county's settlements,
their history, geography, architecture,
industry and curiosities. Also included
are detailed lists of almost everything
from castles and moated mansions to
night clubs: many pages of detailed
indices; biographies of local worthies,
and a most useful glossary of
architectural terms. Shropshire is a lovely
county and here she is explored in her
every nook and cranny. For the author
this book has bitter sweet memories. His
constant and ever chee4rful companion
on his travels was Lady, a cross-bred
Border Collie. On the 27th of September
1989 she and her two daughters, Foxy
and Queenie, disappeared from Mr
Raven's cottage and have never been
seen or heard of again. Mr Raven was,
and still is, heartbroken. 264 pages, A4
size, 196 photographs, sewn in sections
with laminated cover.

Black Country Towns and Villages
Michael Raven
Price £8
A comprehensive gazetteer of the area.
"What makes this book so special is the
quality of the photographs. They are truly
splendid. Michael Raven has the eye
which can see beauty in the
commonplace, the dismal and the
devastated and the skill to communicate
it to the rest of us." John Ogden, Express
and Star.

Shropshire Portraits
Michael Raven
Price £7.50
Black and white photographs of
Shropshire villages and landscapes. Each
picture has an informative caption of
about 75 words. This book was designed
as a companion to A Shropshire
Gazetteer and there is no duplication of
pictures. 64 pages, A4 landscape.

Midlands Digest
Michael Raven
Price £5 each
A series of six magazine style books.
Articles on the curiosities, beauties,
humour and scandals of the area. Heavy
art paper, sewn in sections, 64 pages, A5
size. "Keep up the good work." Sunday
Times.

A Guide to Herefordshire
Michael Raven
Price £20
The latest of my big gazetteers. Richly
illustrated with black and white and
colour photographs and the stunning
scraper board 'etchings' of Hereford
artist Peter Manders. The historian, Roy
Palmer, said of this book: "Michael
Raven's A Guide to Herefordshire is a
magnificent work and not likely to be
surpassed for several generations."
Everything from recently collected
folksongs to the SAS. 256 pages, 12 x 9
inches, sewn in sections with
laminated cover.

Cheshire in Pictures
Michael Raven
Price £7
A mixture of old and new black and
white photographs and period prints
selected for either their artistic merit or
curiosity value. 80 pages, 9 inches by 12
inches, sewn in sections with laminated
cover.

Shropshire in Pictures
Michael Raven
Price £8
A mixture of old and new black and
white photographs and period prints,
selected for either their artistic merit or
curiosity value. Has a rare drawing of the
original castle at Bishop's Castle, found
in the papers of Clive of India. 96 pages,
9 x 12 inches, sewn in sections with
laminated cover.

CD RECORDINGS

Of Michael Raven and Joan Mills
All priced at £12 post free
Complete contents are listed

Songs and Solos
MR68
Michael Raven and Joan Mills:
For Alan Green, Flowers in Her Hair,
Nottingham Swing/Bushes and Briars,
Octopus Dancing, Winifred's
Dream/Winifred's Jig, Lament for Owain
Glyndwr (Sons of Glyndwr), Slender
Boy/Waterloo Dance, Irish Girl, Bunch
of Rushes, Land of Lost Content,
Vyrnwy Waters, Mirror of My Mind,
Prelude in G/Mishca's Restaurant, Pretty
Ploughboy, Lament for Peter
Bellamy/Fred Jordan's Galliard, Waiting
for Wages, Mainstone Hornpipe/Byrne's
Hornpipe, Song of the Fox, Gisburn
Lament/John of Paris/Bird on the Wing,
Midnight City, Lion Cafe/Seth Brown's
Polkas, Lazy Jane, Kirton Grove/Dr
Fauster's Tumblers, Schoon Lief,
Newcastle/A Trip to Scarborough,
WidowWoman's Daughter.

A Shropshire Lad
MR69
Michael Raven and Joan Mills
On Wenlock Edge the Wood's in trouble,
Megan's Daughter, Bredon Hill, Rhoslan
Reel, Half Moon, White Rose of
Summer, New Mistress, Galaru/
The Blackbird, Along the Fields, Long
Live Mary, Is My Team Ploughing?
Bard's Dream, Ludlow Recruit, Megan
who Lost her Garter, Come Pipe a Tune,
Lady Mine/Gogerddan, Midnights of
November, Rising of the Lark/Weep not
for me, True Lover, Beside the
Seashore/Good Ale, Goldcup Flowers,
Where are you going? The Deserter,
Clover, Loitering with a Vacant Eye,
Lady Owen's Delight, Farewell to Barn
and Stack and Tree, My Lady is more
Fair, Wenlock Edge, Snowdon, When I
was One and Twenty, Farewell to
Llangyfelach, Shrewsbury Jail.

Recital
MR70
Michael Raven and Joan Mills
Lass from the Low Country, Queen's
March, Ruth Ellis, Fortune My Foe,
Brinkof the White Rock, Blackbird Wilt
Thy Go?, Green Bushes, Lark's Elegy,
Dancing Delilah, Cafe Cantrell, Hampton
Lullaby, Black is the Colour, Brisk
Young Widow,Come Live with Me,
Minuet de la Cour, Charlie's Song,
Zambra Mora (Pavan for a Dead
Princess), Hednesford Town, Chattering
Magpie, Moorlough Shore,
Pennsylvanian Song/ Captain Heapy,
Biker's Song, The Dove, Illic Jacet,
Alman, Raglan Road

Taming the Dragon's Strings
MR71
*Michael Raven, solo guitar, and some
poetry readings with Joan Mills as guest
on two songs: Loveliest of Trees and The
West.*
Lovely on the Water, Hills of Sarajevo,
Dark Lane, Now All is Still, Raven's
Nest, Christmas at Soulton Hall, Café
Noir, Spanish Morris, Foxy's Flying and
27 September 1989, Almost Slain, Dead
of Rajistan, Melody of Mona, Allurement
of the Pipe, William Philip's Delight,
Saint Bride's Anon, You Must Come to
Kilpeck, Stained Glass, Food for Dogs,
Sarah Collins, Road to Lisdoonvarna,
The West, Linhope, Tome Cave's
Number Three, Sad the Day, Market
Rasen Quickstep, Pell Well Hall, Wild
Bird Weeping, Little Dog Sleeping,
Midsummer Hill, Polly Gale's
Tarantella, I Can Remember, Cidery
Wine, Dark-haired Daughters, Singing
Bird, The Bard's Love, Loveliest of
Trees, Captain's Apprentice, Tobago
Bound, Dark Invader, Dead Elm, Teapot
Time, My Lady's Mood is Quick to
Change, Now All is Still, Lady
Coventry's Minuet, But He Would,
Before I Come Again, Summer's End,
My Last Farewell.

Reynardine Tapes
MR72
*Michael Raven and Joan Mills with
John Rose and Ado Morris*
Brewer's Lady, December Day Dance,
Queen of the Night, Star of Belle Isle,
Greek Street, Old Dublin Fireman,
Lichfield Greenhill Bower Processional,
Three Hearty Young Poachers, The
Castle/Tulla Reel, Stafford Pageant
Song, White Copper Alley, Trent
Waters/Marion's Rambles, Johnny
Gallagher, Eternal Father, Lord Thomas,

Lakes of Pontchatrain, Poor Law Bill, Hungarian Hat, Crafty Maid's Policy, Maid on the Shore/Black Mountain/Gaunt Man, Sally Gardens, Tarantos.

Flowers of Picardy
MR73
Michael Raven and Joan Mills
Flowers of Picardy, Sicilian Waltz, Epitaph on an Army of Mercenaries, La Russe Waltz, Paris Polka, Dancing Lady, Green Fields of England, Robin Hood's Dance, Maid of Provence, Stafford County Fair, Trecynon Polka, Over the Wall, New Tenpenny Bit, My Last Farewell to Stirling, Carrickfergus, Bentley Canal, With Measured Sound, Adson's Sarabande, Cluster of Nuts, Mallorca, Oh, Fair Enough, Cypress Curtain, Mrs. Anne Harcourt's Galliard, Robin Hood and the Tanner, Rhododendron, The Singer, The Old Soldier, The Backwoodsman, March to Kandahar, The Unknown Grave.

Welsh Guitar
MR74
Michael Raven, solo guitar
Grey Cuckoo, Sailor's Grave/You Carefree Young Lads, Honied Kiss/Glwysen, Sweet Richard, Rheadr Falls, Rising of the Sun, The Harp, Rheged/Lady Treffael's Conceit, Miller's Song/Over the Stone, Honied Lip, Men of Wrexham's Hornpipe, Glenbargoed, Farewell Marian, Machynlleth, The Judgement/Old Year Passing, Spanish Minuet/Maids of Montgomery, Tretower Waltz, John Francis, Llanberis Pass, Flowers of the Thorn, Maltraeth, Watching the Wheat/Gwenllian, Captain Morgan's March/Lady Sker, Gwenllian's Repose, Come What May/Glandyfi, Fanny Blooming Fair, Weep not for Me, Ap Siencyn/Abergynolwen, The Blackbird, Llangoffen, My Love is a Venus, Springtime is Returning, Welsh Rabbit/Llyn Gwernan, Missing Boat, Corn -thresher Hornpipe, Clover of Merioneth, Once a Farmer.

Retrospective
MR75 (includes Gipsy, A Variety of Guitar Music, (Cambrian SCLP 610)
Michael Raven, solo guitar
Dark Eyes, Farruca, Staines Morris,

Zarabanda, Mistress Winter's Jump, Soleares, Guido's Rag, Melancholy Pavan, Willow Rag, Lichfield Bower Processional, Vals by Aguado, Rhumba Cubana, Lady Mary, Argent, Going with David to Towyn, Bolero, Fandango de Almeria, Chula, Over the Stone, Rakes of Mallow, Tanguillio, Prelude, Warrior's Welcome Home, Comical Fellow, Bushes and Briars, Two Butchers Sirtos, Sarabande, Fanfare, Hymn, Waltz, Helston Furry Dance, Midnights of November, A Jigg Ashling, Ladies Go Dancing at Whitsun, Beatrice Hill's Reel/Morpeth Rant, Dowland's Alman, Please to See the King, Off to California, Poor Murdered Woman/Clee Hill Reel.

Songs and Dances of Herefordshire
MR76
Michael Raven and Joan Mills with Pat and Roy Palmer as guests
Lowlands of Holland, Jack Gore's Galliard, Dives and Lazarus, Mr. Baskerville's Volt, Foolish Boy, Hunting the Squirrel, Banks of Sweet Primroses, Ledbury Timber-Teams, Orange in Bloom, Rich Old Lady, Holywell, Trees they do Grow High, John Locke's Polka, My Mother Bid Me, Barbara Ellen, Milkmaid's Song, Restless Road, Speed the Plough, Sheffield Park, Jack of the Green, Thundermanshire, Moon Shines Bright, The Blacksmith, Leaves of Life, London Town, Sheepskins, Rose in June, Blue-Eyed Stranger, Oh Who is That?, Cider Annie, Piers Ploughman, Herefordshire Lasses, Ledbury Parson.

The Jolly Machine
MR77
Michael Raven and Joan Mills with Saga. See TheHalliard:Jon Raven
Chartists' Anthem, Nailmakers' Lament, Charlie's Song, Redditch Needlemakers' Lament, Landlord Don't You Cry, Freedom and Reform, Potter's Chant, Waiting for Wages, Wednesbury Town, Jolly Machine, Colliers' Rant, John Whitehouse, Tommy Note, Dudley Canal Tunnel Song.

The Halliard:Jon Raven
MR77 (Originally on Broadside)
One of two LP re-releases on a single CD with the Jolly Machine

Calico Printer's Clerk, Unquiet Grave, Ladies Don't Go a-Theivin', Midsummer Fair, To the Weavers Gin Ye, Long Lankin, Going for a Soldier Jenny, Workhouse Boy, Row Bullies Row, Lancashire Lads, A Thousand Miles Away, Love and Murder, Last Farewell, Jolly Joe, Rambling Sailor

My Old Friend
MR80
Michael Raven and Joan Mills with guest, Johnny Collins
Has a 36 page booklet with the music to all of the songs and guitar solos.
My Old Friend, Errol Flynn, Abbot's Bromley Horn Dance, Song for Diana, Because I Liked you Better, Sheba's Daughter, Che Geuvara, Is my Dear Lord Asleep?, Squire Mytton's Gallop, English Lanes, John Collins, The Rebel Leader's Lament, Grey Valley, Maid from the Northlands, Queen of the Night, My Bonny Lads Away, Loveliest of Trees, Spanish Morris.

CASSETTE COMPILATIONS
All priced at £7.00

The Folk Heritage Recordings
Michael Raven (guitar)
Joan Mills (vocals & guitar)
Selected tracks from the LP Death and the Lady (1972): Jolly Highwayman, Lisa Lan, Ladies Don't Go a Thieving, Robin Hood's Dance, Sarabande, Captain's Apprentice, Can y Melinydd, Troseg y Gareg, Sarah Collins, White Gloves, La Russe Waltz, Paris Polka, Queen of the Night. Selected tracks from the LP Hymn to Che Guevara (1974): Belle Star and Jesse James, Twenty Years, Melancholy Pavan, Hymn to Che Guevara, Great Train Robbery, Magpies in Picardy, Little White Donkey, Dancing Lady, Midnight City. 60 minutes playing time. Available as cassette only.

A Miscellany of Guitar Music
Broadside KBRO 124
Michael Raven
Recorded in 1977 on the Broadside Label. Contents: Suite in D: Prelude, Warrior's Welcome Home, Comical Fellow, Bushes and Briars, Two Butchers; Leonore, Aymara, McKinnon's Lament and Jig, New Mown Hay, Bourree, Rough Music. Suite in E: Sarabande, Fanfare, Hymn Waltz; Lakes of Pontchetrain Jonathan Wild's Jig, Tarantos, Black Joke, To the Weavers. Available as either LP record or cassette.

Celtic Flamenco
MR78
Michael Raven, solo guitar
A cassette consisting of tracks taken from CD recordings of flamenco and flamenco inspired arrangements of British tunes. The contents are: Troseg y Gareg/Rakes of Mallow/Tanguillio, Chattering Magpie, Lovely on the Water/Hills of Sarajevo, Lichfield Bower Processional, Willow Rag, Soleares, Black is the Colour, Bolero, Road to Lisdoonvarna/Road to Towyn, Maid of Provence, Spanish Morris

The Irish In Me
MR79
Joan Mills with Michael Raven
Joan's mother,"Jeannie" Meehan, came from Ballindrait, Donegal. The contents are: Maid from the Northlands, Errol Flynn, Sally Gardens, The Backwoodsman, Old Dublin Fireman, Johnny Gallagher, Moorlough Shore. Widow Woman's Daughter, Brink of the White Rock, Star of Belle Isle, Irish Girl, Raglan Road. 46 minutes playing time. Cassette only.

LP RECORDS SINGLES AND CASSETTES NOW DELETED
These LPs are now deleted and only available in the market place where they are very expensive – £250 plus in the case of Death and the Lady

Death and the Lady
Folk Heritage Recordings FHR 047
Michael Raven and Joan Mills
Death and the Lady, The Jolly Highwayman, Lisa Lan, Ladies Don't Go a-Thievin', Robin Hood's Dance, Staines Morris/La Folia Saraband/Adson's Saraband, Saraband, The Lichfield Greenhill Bower Processional, The Captain's Apprentice, Can y Melinydd/Troseg y Gareg, Sarah Collins, The White Gloves, La Russe Waltz/Paris Polka, The Queen of the Night.

Hymn to Che Guevara
Folk Heritage Recordings FHR 054
Michael Raven and Joan Mills
Belle Starr and Jesse James, Twenty
Years, Tim Evans' Dance, Melancholy
Pavanne, Perry Mason's Maggot, Hymn
to Che Geuvara, The Great Train
Robbery, Magpies in Picardy, Little
White Donkey, Dancing Lady, Over the
Wall, Midnight City.

Can y Melinydd
Munich Records MU 7430
Michael Raven and Joan Mills
Katie Cruel, Maid of Tottenham, Owain
Glyndwr, Tenpenny Jig, Bedlam Boys,
Constant Lover, Clerk Colvill, Burning
of Auchindown, Brisk young Widow,
Night Visiting Song, Young Jane/ Lord
McDonald's Reel, Brave Nelson, Widow
Woman's Daughter, Can y Melinydd
(The Miller's Song).

Kate of Coalbrookdale
Argo (Decca) ZFB 29
*Michael Raven, Jon Raven and Jean
Ward with Pete Sage (fiddle)*
Brisk Young Butcher, I wish, I Wish,
Brave Collier Lads, Buxom Young
Dairymaid, Kate of Coalbrookdale, Cold
Blows thw Wind, Wife for Sale,
Soldier's Fancy, Bold William Taylor,
Rose of Cashmere, Nine Times a Night,
Collier Lass, Pirate's Serenade, The Grey
Cock.

**Songs of the Black Country and West
Midlands**
Broadside BRO 100
*Michael Raven, Jon Raven
and Jean Ward*
King Henry and the King of France, Bold
Robin Hood, The Rose Tree, Cold Blows
the Wind, Come all Yew Blades, Brave
Collier Lads, Collier Lass, Ballad of
Trubshaw and Green, Wife for Sale,
Nailmakers''Strike, Wedgebury Cocking,
Gabriels Hounds, John Wesley, William
Booth, Darlaston Dogfight, Staffordshire
Hornpipe, Hampton Lullaby,
Ye three Tall Men.

The Black Country Three
Transatlantic TRA 140
Michael & Jon Raven with Derek Craft
Boxing Match, Long Ago, Far Away,
Buttermilk Hill, Song of the Western

Men, Three Ravens, Jolly Joe, Row
Bullies Row, Wedgefield Wake,
Villancico, Wine of Gaul, She Moved
Through the Fair, Mission of San
Miguel, Riflemen of Bennington, All
Bells in Paradise.

Che Guevara
Big Bear BB 31 (single)
Michael Raven and Joan Mills
Che Guevara, Devil's Dance.

Sarah's Song
Philips 60060121 (single)
Joan Mills with Heritage
Sarah's Song, Long Way Home

Michael Raven and Joan Mills
Cassette with no catalogue number
*Michael Raven and Joan Mills with
David Oxley, John Caven and
Mark Wallis*
Yarmouth Tragedy, Green Fields of
England, Cluster of Nuts, Captain
Bellew's Dance, Fair Land, Tobago
Bound (with Reynardine), Queen of
theMay, Black Friar's Reel, Stafford
Pageant Song, You Rambling Boys of
Pleasure, Kitty O'Lynn, Stafford County
Fair, Sicilian Waltz, Farewell to Stirling,
Carrick Fergus, Maid and the Box, Little
Field of Barley, Willie O'Winsbury,
March to Kandahar.

Guitar Magic
Transatlantic TRA XTRA 1046
Michael Raven, solo guitar

The Black Country Three
Wolverhampton Folksong Club EP
*Michael Raven, Jon Raven and
Derek Craft*
Boxing Match, Clemeny, Nailmakers'
Strike, Dudley Canal Tunnel Song

Lass from the Low Country
Roman Head RH 021
Michael Raven and Jean Ward

The Dutch Connection
Cassette with no catalogue number
Michael Raven and Joan Mills

Gipsy: A Variety of Guitar Music
Cambrian SCLP 610
(see Retrospective CD)
Michael Raven, solo guitar

Review in **Folk Roots** of Michael Raven and Joan Mills' *Songs and Solos* MRCD68

Get past the forbidding cover shot and you will find something quite exceptional. Raven is a guitarist of unquestionable but carefully controlled virtuosity and Mills has the heretical idea that you can successfully sing folksongs in your own, everyday unaffected voice.

Pretty well everything here is either traditional or of Raven's making. He's arranged it all including a couple of A. E. Housman poems, and not put a foot wrong as far as I'm concerned. The instrumentals use a lot of technique and harmonic development more commonly found on the flamenco and classical guitar than in the folk arena but what comes through, rather than any flashiness, is his sheer command of the instrument and his material.

Joan Mills sings in an immediately attractive voice and sparing use of decoration, sensitively accompanied by Raven's guitar. Her unforced, natural approach is absolutely fine by me, especially on Irish Girl and Widow Woman's Daughter. She does just enough to put the songs across, not imposing herself any further than that. This economy of approach extends to the avoidance of editing and multi-tracking - they seem to cope perfectly well without. *Nick Beale*

Review in **Folk North-West** of Michael Raven and Joan Mills' *Songs and Solos* MRCD68

Mike Raven has been researching and writing books about folk music, writing tunes for guitar and generally immersing himself in 'the music' for many, many years. He is, as a result, a well-respected authority on a wide range of musical styles. For some time this work has restricted his opportunities to perform on the folk club circuit, so, it was with some delight that I recently received this CD featuring Mike and his singing partner, Joan.

The performances here are quite idiosyncratic but nevertheless classic in every respect. Mike's guitar work is stunning in its intricacy, combining classical and folk styles in a fusion of complex tunes, many of which are self-penned. Joan's superb voice is clear and crystal-like reflecting her Irish connections and is matched superbly by Mike's meticulous arrangements.

There is no hype or recording trickery here and the result is as near a perfect reproduction of a live performance as it is possible to achieve. This is music that demands your attention and rightly deserves it. *Derek Gifford*

Index

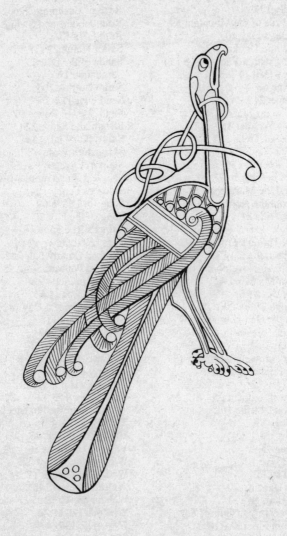